• *Creative Bible Learning Series* •

Everything You Want to Know About
Teaching Young Children

BIRTH–6 YEARS

Wesley Haystead

GL
Gospel Light
Publications

Published by Regal Books
A Division of GL Publications
Ventura, California 93006
Printed in U.S.A.

The Scripture quotations unless otherwise noted are from:
The Holy Bible: The New International Version. Copyright © 1973, 1978, 1984
International Bible Society. Used by permission of Zondervan Bible Publishers.
Other versions quoted are:
NASB—New American Standard Bible. © The Lockman Foundation 1960,
     1962, 1963, 1968, 1971, 1972, 1973, 1975. Used by permission.
TLB—From *The Living Bible,* Copyright © 1971 by Tyndale House Publishers,
     Wheaton, Illinois. Used by permission.
Bible verses that have been edited for ease of understanding by young children
     are indicated by "See" along with the reference. E.g., (See Galatians 6:10.)

Library of Congress Cataloging in publication data

Haystead, Wesley.
     Everything you want to know about teaching young children / Wesley
     Haystead.
          p.   cm.
     Bibliography: p.
     ISBN 0-8307-1272-0 :
     1. Christian education of children—Handbooks, manuals, etc.
I. Title.
BV1475.2.H39   1989
268'.432   dc19

1 2 3 4 5 6 7 8 9 10 / 91 90 89

Rights for publishing this book in other languages are contracted by
Gospel Literature International (GLINT) foundation. GLINT also provides
technical help for the adaptation, translation, and publishing of Bible
study resources and books in scores of languages worldwide. For further
information, contact GLINT, Post Office Box 488, Rosemead, California,
91770, U.S.A., or the publisher.

The publishers do not necessarily endorse the entire contents of all publications
referred to in this book.

Contents

The Author

Wesley Haystead is a Christian Education specialist. He received his Master's degree in educational psychology from the University of Southern California and has been working with children, teaching them, and writing for them for more than 20 years. He served as the Minister of Education for churches in Oregon and California. He worked at Gospel Light Publications for 12 years, serving as the Early Childhood Coordinator for the International Center for Learning seminars and, for five years, as the Senior Editor of the Curriculum Division.

Currently, Wesley is Editorial Director at Lowell Brown Enterprises. He is the father of three children. He and his wife, Sheryl, live in Ventura, California, where they are coordinators for the children's Sunday School department (birth through fifth grade) at their church.

Preface

Gospel Light Publications is committed to obeying Christ's command to "go and make disciples ... teaching them" (Matt. 28:19,20). To fulfill this great commission, Gospel Light provides in-depth training resources for leaders ministering in churches of all sizes. Gospel Light helps teachers discover how to motivate students to be involved in learning the life-changing truths of God's Word.

This book is designed for both the new teacher and those who are more experienced. Wesley Haystead concisely presents the needs and characteristics of young children. He will help you discover a variety of ways you can provide effective Bible learning. These insights into your learners and the learning process will enable you to make the Bible come alive for your young learners.

You can profit from reading this book alone and discussing it with a group of teachers. You will want to refer to this book many times for assistance in planning new methods and programs as well as improving what you are already doing.

PART 1

The Young Child and Learning

The Young Child in the 21st Century

It was a clear fall morning and I was playing hooky from work. I had mumbled an excuse to my co-workers about an important appointment and left the office. Even though I had started work early that morning, I felt just a little guilty about the pile of work I had left on my desk. A few minutes later, any lingering remorse vanished when I pulled up in front of my house and saw five-year-old Jonathan waiting at the curb with his bicycle. I had promised him that this was the morning he would finally ride without training wheels.

The removal of training wheels is an important rite of passage in any family. It is usually accomplished with a child announcing the event to the neighborhood, a father muttering about whoever put the nuts on so tightly, and a mother worriedly asking if it wouldn't be better to wait another month or year or two.

Jonathan and I packed his bike into the trunk of the car and drove to a large city park with a gently curving walkway bounded on both sides by lots of soft grass. My plan was to jog along beside the bike, using one hand to steady it if needed. The plan had worked beautifully with Karen and Andrew in earlier years, so there was no doubt in my mind it would work again.

However, after repeated wobbly jaunts around the park, doubts were emerging with each puff. "I'm too old for this," I wheezed. "I'll never last long enough for him to catch on." After several near misses with strategically placed trees, I slumped onto a park bench and whispered, "Time out, Jonathan."

Then I looked at his face. He had the determined look of a warrior. His jaw was set, his teeth were bared, his eyes were bright. As my glasses fogged from my sweat, I heard his voice: "Let's go, Dad! I'm ready!"

What could I do? How could I give up? I couldn't face the specter of letting him down. So, off we lurched, terrifying an elderly lady and her dog, careening from one side of the path to the other. And then Jonathan pulled ahead of me and kept on going. He was off!

Perhaps it was my exhausted state, but I stood in the middle of the path watching my youngest child pedal away from me and I cried. A moment ago he had needed my hand on his back and now he was on his own. So quickly he had moved from dependence to independence, from insecurity to security, from uncertainty to confidence. Now my glasses were really fogged as I confronted the joy and the sadness of helping to launch a child into the stream of human experience.

As a teacher of young children, you are helping to launch youngsters toward new understandings, new experiences, new relationships—and toward a new century! How do we help prepare a little one to become God's person in a rapidly changing society? What will the children we teach need in order to fulfill God's purpose for their lives as the calendar leads us into a new millennium? Launching a child on a bicycle is relatively simple, if exhausting. Launching a child into the future is fraught with countless unknowns.

Many people enjoy speculating about changes that will occur in the 21st century. Experts in a wide variety of fields study today's trends and attempt to predict where they will lead in the future. Rather than trying to forecast the uncertainties of the future, consider what we do know about the nature of the child and the command Christ gave concerning the child.

JESUS AND CHILDREN

It was very obvious to everyone in the room that the topic being discussed was of great importance to Jesus. Earlier in the day He had withstood another attempt of the Pharisees to trap Him. They had raised the question of divorce and Jesus had responded with some truly startling statements.

The disciples were full of questions and could hardly wait until they reached the privacy of the house to begin asking Jesus about the things He had said. Jesus was in the middle of His explanation when the door opened and some people brought their children to have Jesus touch them.

Every usher in every church I know would have done exactly what Jesus' disciples did that day. They quietly began herding these parents and their children back out the door, explaining firmly that Jesus was in the middle of a very important discussion and should not be interrupted by children. Isn't that what the ushers in your church would do if you brought your class of young children up to the platform in the middle of your pastor's sermon?

The disciples' problem—one that all of us as adults share— was that they assumed an important (even urgent) adult discussion took precedence over a noisy group of children. They—and we—put more value on adults than on youngsters, more worth on issues than on persons.

How did Jesus respond to what his disciples were doing? "He was indignant" (Mark 10:14). Jesus commanded His followers not to turn away children who came to Him. Children have a place in His Kingdom. God loves infants as much as He loves adults, and toddlers as much as teenagers.

It is true that the first five years of life leave a child far short of adult understandings, skills and responsibilities. However, the child is still equipped with an amazing array of capacities that make thoughtful, loving ministry a necessity. Every teacher, parent, pastor and congregation that seriously wants to follow Jesus' example in the world must be concerned about children. A church must share Jesus' deep respect for a child, sensing the great value God places on each one.

WHY TEACH BIBLE TRUTHS TO YOUNG CHILDREN?

God's long-range goal for every child and adult is for them to reach "the knowledge of the Son of God and become mature, attaining to the whole measure of the fullness of Christ" (Eph. 4:13). The earliest beginnings of this great process can occur while the child is still a babe in arms, being loved by people who love God.

Timothy was reminded that, as a child, he understood and responded to Bible truths which "make you wise for salvation through faith in Christ Jesus" (2 Tim. 3:15).

Just as Timothy's boyhood introduction to Scripture began his preparation for a life of service, children today need the same opportunity, both at home and at church.

First, we teach the Bible to children in order that at God's appointed time, as the Holy Spirit guides, the child will express faith in the Lord Jesus Christ as Savior, becoming a member of God's family. Jesus said, "You must be born again" (John 3:7).

But, like physical birth, this experience is part of a process. A baby must develop in the womb before birth. Jesus compared the preparation of the heart to the planting of seed which later bears fruit. Ideas and attitudes that take root in the child will produce a rich harvest in years that follow. Most conversions among children are recorded between the ages of 10 and 12. However, the child who attends Sunday School during the early years— and particularly if from a supportive Christian home—often is capable of an earlier, meaningful response to Jesus' love. A child needs to be nurtured in the things of God in order to develop a personal faith.

Second, Bible truths help the child discern right from wrong, building a foundation for truly Christian values. For example, the

Bible command, "Be kind" (Eph. 4:32), takes on real meaning for two-year-old David when we help him to wait his turn to paint, and then praise him for obeying God's Word: "Waiting your turn to paint is a good way to 'be kind,' David, just like the Bible says." Children's values are formed by example and supported by words. The child constantly watches adults' attitudes and actions, imitating their behavior. The child seeks adult approval for that behavior. When this behavior is clearly associated with Bible truth, it becomes even more important to the child to continue that action. The process of connecting Bible statements to desired behaviors and attitudes is one important step in building a foundation for Christian values in a child's life.

Third, Bible truths help a child develop a biblical awareness of the world. The child needs to feel that his or her experiences are all a part of God's loving plan and care. Children need the security that such a realization can bring. It was a moment of great wonder and comfort for Andrea when her teacher finished thanking God for the morning snack, then said, "God hears us when we talk to Him. He listens because He loves us. The Bible tells us 'God cares for you'" (see 1 Pet. 5:7). Such experiences bear fruit as the child's understanding is quickened by the Holy Spirit. The child who learns to believe in and count on God's unchanging love will develop healthy feelings of personal worth.

Fourth, the young child who becomes familiar with ways Scriptures apply to life, develops a positive, receptive attitude to the Bible. The child learns that it is desirable to obey the commands of God and be strengthened by His promises.

Young children live in a world of immediacy. Their concern is for what is happening here and now. Teachers and parents who relate Bible truth to current experiences appeal to the child's need to find God at work in every area of life today.

HOW DOES A YOUNG CHILD THINK?

1. The young child thinks literally and concretely. ■

Abstract and symbolic ideas will always be taken in their literal, physical sense. Five-year-old Monica demonstrated this when she stopped saying her bedtime prayers the week her family moved to a new house. Monica's mother thought her daughter must have been deeply upset by being uprooted. However, Monica showed every outward sign of being perfectly happy in her new home and neighborhood. Not for several weeks did her parents discover the real cause of her reluctance to pray. In her previous house, located just around the corner from her church, it was very easy for her to visualize her prayers being heard by God, who in her mind was around the corner in His "house." When they moved across town, her faith would not stretch far enough to imagine that God could still hear her. Her literal thinking had created images of God living in the church building and audibly listening to the words of her prayers.

2. The young child's thinking grows out of personal experience. ■ The child knows what he or she has seen and done. Words alone are very imperfect conveyers of information. The child needs a frame of reference in order for verbal explanations to make any sense. The child's need for experience is often revealed in connection with the next limitation on the child's thinking—vocabulary.

3. The young child's thinking is limited by vocabulary. ■ A three-year-old child is capable of understanding 85-90 percent of normal adult conversation. But the unfamiliar words in the other 10-15 percent crop up often enough to create problems. Rarely does a child under four ask for an explanation of an unfamiliar word. The child is much too busy learning everything to have time to ask for definitions. Instead, the child develops a pattern of fitting unknown words into something that is already known.

One Easter Sunday we were driving home from church and I asked Andrew what his Bible story had been about. It seemed like a safe question to ask on Easter. He responded enthusiastically, "It was about Jesus in prison."

I knew enough about the Bible to know stories about Paul in prison and Joseph in prison, but I hadn't heard one about Jesus in prison. After a few more questions, it suddenly became clear what Andrew had really heard. All morning long, teachers had been talking about "Jesus is risen!" They had sung songs about it, thanked God for it, told children to be glad because of it. But no one had ever stopped to explain what "risen" means. Never having heard the word before, Andrew simply did what most young children do. He substituted a word that sounded similar, and spent the whole morning wondering why everyone was so happy that Jesus was in prison.

Even when children use the correct word, there is no guarantee they know what it means. Young children are very skilled at imitating, so they sing songs, quote verses, use expressions and figures of speech and often have no idea at all what they just sang or said. And it does not bother them one bit that they do not understand. They are like some politicians: perfectly content to hear themselves talking whether they make sense or not.

4. The young child's thinking is shaped by a limited point of view. ■ While adults often have trouble accepting someone else's point of view, children get in trouble because they are not even aware anyone could have a different outlook on things. The child blithely assumes everyone shares exactly the same thoughts and feelings about everything.

Thus, once a young child has gotten a fix on an idea, it is very hard to change his or her mind. If there's only one way of looking at things, the child must be right.

The child's point of view will also produce some interesting conclusions because he or she will often focus attention on some minor or irrelevant matter and miss the essential components. For example, a young child is as likely to tell you the story of the Good Samaritan is about donkeys or bandages or robbers as it is about showing kindness to someone in need. If the donkey captured the child's attention, then to the child the story is about a donkey.

HOW CAN WE TEACH
BIBLE TRUTHS TO YOUNG CHILDREN?

Guiding children in their early years is an awesome task. The importance of helping children learn basic scriptural truth cannot be overemphasized. Fortunately, God has not left us to accomplish this task in our own strength. He offers us the instruction of the Holy Spirit and the promise of His guidance: "If you want to know what God wants you to do, ask him, and he will gladly tell you, for he is always ready to give a bountiful supply of wisdom to all who ask him; he will not resent it" (Jas. 1:5, *TLB*).

With this assurance of guidance how does one go about teaching little ones of God's love? What methods and techniques will communicate the Bible truth in terms that a child can understand?

1. Focus on relationships. ■ Because the young child learns more from who you are than what you say, you must consider the child before the content and demonstrate caring before you communicate ideas. Until you love the child, the child is not ready to listen to you.

2. Provide first-hand experiences. ■ Because the young child's ability to think depends on what he or she has done, you must provide the child with many opportunities to touch, taste, smell, see and hear. Because the child is not yet able to play with ideas, you must guide him or her to play with materials. While adults consider play as a frivolous activity, something to engage in after our work is finished, the young child's world contains no such distinction. Play and work are identical—and it is through play that the young child most effectively learns.

3. Look for "teachable moments." ■ In the midst of the child's play come moments of curiosity, of expectation, of pleasure, of frustration. It is in the moment of heightened interest that the child is most receptive to a new idea, or the security of a familiar truth. As the child paints or builds with blocks or tucks a doll in bed, a teacher looks for the moment when the child is open to a brief exchange of ideas.

4. Add descriptive conversation. ■ When the teachable moment occurs, the alert teacher is ready with a comment, linking the child's activity to Bible words and events. A Bible verse spoken while a child is putting together a puzzle can be understood and remembered better than the same verse spoken while the child sits quietly on a chair. You will be most effective when you bring the Bible to the child, rather than trying to bring the child to the Bible.

5. Ask questions related to activity. ■ Often a question will stimulate thinking more than a direct comment. Questions (except those that can be answered "Yes," "No," "Jesus" or "God") involve the child in dialog with the teacher, and encourage the child to think of how the activity illustrates a truth from God's Word.

6. Answer questions. ■ If children are thinking, they are asking questions. The answers you give are highly significant in helping the child's understanding to grow. Sometimes adults condescend to a child's questions (especially the highly philosophical ones that four- and five-year-olds love to ask about the meaning of life and the nature of God), assuming the child cannot really handle a correct answer. This is when parents suddenly change the subject or invent a story about a stork.

At other times, adults sense an opening and attempt to deposit the wisdom of the ages on the unsuspecting child. As one who has a tendency to tell people how to make watches when all they want is to know the time, it has been a sometimes painful process learning not to tell everything I know on a subject just because a child was foolhardy enough to ask a question.

Karen was five years old when she taught me this lesson for the first time. While I was driving across town, she asked me a very significant question (which neither she nor I can recall).

Thrilled at her interest I answered her. And I answered her. And I kept on answering all the way across town. Finally, while stopped at a red light, I looked in the rear view mirror to see how well my answers were being received by the fair young seeker after truth, but she was nowhere to be seen. Quickly, I looked over my shoulder and found her hunched down on the floor of the car with her hands over her ears! So much for the advantages of having a dad who writes books about young children!

The child who asks a one-sentence question, expects a one-sentence answer. And the child deserves that answer to be as simple and honest as the adult can make it. Once that is done, it is a perfectly sound practice to ask if the child would like to know more about the question. If so, add a little more information, taking your cues from the child's further questions.

When the child asks a truly hard question (Why did Grandma die? Why does God let bad things happen? Where is heaven? How can Jesus be God's Son?), no damage is inflicted by admitting the limits of your own knowledge. Even if a child is frustrated by your inadequate explanation of eternity, you can do a great deal of good by reminding the child that God is so great, no one can understand all about Him or the things He does. If I knew the answers to all the questions children have asked me, I would be as smart as God, and even the youngest children I teach know I'm not nearly that smart.

Can your church provide an effective ministry to young children? Can you accept Jesus' concern for little ones? Do you have adults who want to share God's love to help children make a good beginning? The answer to those questions is not a matter of size, finances, programs or facilities. It is a matter of attitude and commitment.

This handbook can help with ideas, with plans, with essential techniques. The help for attitudes and commitment can come only through earnest prayer.

Three stonemasons, when asked what they were doing, replied as follows:

"Laying a stone," said the first.
"Making a wall," said the second.
"Building a cathedral," said the third.

Three Sunday School teachers were asked what they were doing:

"Baby-sitting these kids," said the first.
"Caring for the children," said the second.
"Sharing God's love," replied the third.

The Young Child's Home and Church

Your department can provide a good learning environment and loving atmosphere for young children. But children spend most of their time at home. It is the home that really molds a child. The attitudes of parents, brothers and sisters have far greater impact on the child than do those of the Sunday School teacher who sees the child only one day a week.

Timothy grew up in a home that provided consistent Christian nurture. Both his grandmother and mother had sincere faith. They taught him the sacred writings which gave him wisdom and in turn led to his salvation. They surely must have demonstrated their teachings in their lives, for young children learn by observation and example more than by merely receiving instruction by word of mouth.

Ever since Old Testament times faithful families have been taught to be Bible-centered. This obviously implies more than "reading a chapter" together, one night a week. Parents were to weave the instruction of the Word diligently and naturally throughout all their daily activities. They were to demonstrate, and talk about, Bible truth in relationship to everyday life (see Deut. 6:4-7).

The ministry of the Sunday School is incomplete when it is disassociated from a child's home. Cooperation and mutual support between Sunday School and home are of great value to a child's growth.

You, as a concerned teacher, can be used to help your children's families! You can minister to the child from the non-

Christian family! You can support and encourage young parents who are looking for answers to the challenges of guiding their child! You can encourage the mature Christian parent who may have more experience and understanding than you!

All parents respond to concerned, friendly individuals who reflect God's love for their child. All teachers can benefit from the insights parents have about their own child. A teacher must approach parents, not as one who has all the answers, but as a friend who wants to support them in teaching and helping their child. In this way the teacher truly becomes "a servant," one who follows Jesus' example in offering care and concern.

CONTACT WITH PARENTS ON SUNDAYS

There are many ways to build relationships with the families of those you teach. Your first contact with the parents, when they bring "Jennifer" or "Andy" for the first time, is of extreme importance. Personal interest in both the child and the parents must be shown from the start. Be well-prepared and ready to go at least 15 minutes before Sunday School is scheduled to start. This will make it possible for the Department Leader or a teacher to greet children and parents as they arrive.

At the end of the session, the teacher or leader who is at the door should make friendly, brief comments on each child's activities during the morning. When necessary, to discuss something with the parents, arrange a convenient time for a phone call or visit that week.

Also, look for opportunities to talk briefly with parents at other times around church. Seek them out before or after services. Invite them to sit with you in church. Talk with them about matters other than their child, building gradually stronger bonds of friendship.

HOW CAN OUR DEPARTMENT COMMUNICATE WITH THE HOME?

Personal contacts show that someone cares. They are the indispensible means of developing mutual sharing and appreciation.

Writing

The simplest type of personal contact is a handwritten note, card or letter. Notes should be sent to both the parents and the child. Three-year-olds rarely get mail. Their excitement at receiving a card makes the effort well worthwhile. This type of contact is read at the receiver's convenience, is non-threatening and pleasant. It shows you care and helps build good will. It is only a one-way contact, however, with no opportunity for response. The receiver knows how you feel, but you are unaware of how the message was received.

Phoning

The telephone is also quick and easy to use and allows for conversation. It cannot embarrass anyone because of their personal appearance or the cleanliness of their home. However, the phone can interrupt, catching people at an inconvenient time. A warm voice can quickly set a person at ease and sensitive ears can let you know if you would be better off calling at another time.

Occasionally call to talk with the child. With twos and threes you may get mostly silence at the other end. But both parents and child will appreciate your interest.

Visiting

The first visit in a home should focus on explaining your Sunday School program. Describe the learning methods of the department and the basic theme and aims of the current unit you are teaching. Bring a photo album of pictures of children at work. Also show some typical samples of children's work as well as the take-home paper and student pages provided in the curriculum.

An excellent follow-up is to arrange a visit just to see the child. Explain the value for a child to see you outside the classroom situation. When you come to the home, focus attention on the child rather than the adults. Visit the child's room and favorite toys and engage in child-level conversation. Parents will often become more open, too, as they see their child respond to your interest.

When making a home visit, observe these general guidelines:

1. Have a stated reason for calling—to deliver a gift to a sick child, explain new procedures in the department, etc.

2. Call and make an appointment to insure coming at a convenient time.

3. Make the visit with your spouse or another teacher.

4. Keep your visit brief.

5. Talk about the child's positive behavior.

6. With non-Christian parents, briefly share your relationship with Christ. Invite the parents to attend church or an adult Sunday School class. Leave a church bulletin listing activities.

7. Pray for the child's family before and after each visit.

ORGANIZING FOR HOME CONTACTS

The most important action a department can take to enable teachers to make significant home contacts is to assign each teacher a small group of children—no more than six—for whom the teacher will pray and make follow-up contacts.

An important aid in keeping in touch with children's homes is an accurate system of records. These include the child's name, address, phone number and date of birth. It is helpful to include the names and ages of other family members also.

Be aware of each child's pattern of attendance. The absence of a child on a Sunday morning should trigger some response by the teacher. Usually a phone call is the best contact after the first absence, in order to determine the reason the child was not there. Most parents appreciate a friendly inquiry, such as, "We really missed Jennifer. Is everything OK?" If the child is ill, an appropriate response can be made. To merely send cards when the reason for the absence is not known, may result in missing an opportunity to minister in a time of real need.

Absences should not be the only reason for making a contact. Otherwise, parents and children may sense they are merely objects in attendance-building efforts, not people for whom teachers really care. Birthdays and special events offer good reasons to write or call, or even to invite a child out for a special treat. Keep accurate records on these contacts so that no child is overlooked.

In addition to the general Sunday School records, keep a personal record of the progress of each child in your class. The most obvious growth appears in the areas of physical stature and ability, social interaction and vocabulary skills. Also be aware of each child's development in relation to the Bible aims of your lessons. This evaluation could be done as part of a department planning meeting, with all the teachers contributing their observations on each child. An outline such as the one following can help guide your thinking.

Early Childhood Progress Evaluation

Self-Concept

1. To what extent does child become involved in activity?
2. How does child respond to new experiences?
3. How does child respond to success or failure?

Attitudes Toward Others

1. What skills does child have in participating with a group of children?
2. To what extent does child show sensitivity to the rights of others?
3. How does child respond to small groups of children? Large groups?

Attitudes Toward Church

1. What indication does child give of liking or disliking coming to church?
2. How does child respond toward individual teachers?
3. Is child's attendance pattern improving or decreasing?

Attitude Toward Bible and Prayer

1. How does child respond to conversation about Bible verses?

2. How does child respond to invitation to hear a Bible story?

3. How does child respond in moments of prayer and worship?

Feelings Toward Jesus

1. What statements has child made that reflect understanding of Jesus?

2. What evidence does child give of feeling that Jesus is a good friend?

3. How often does child spontaneously introduce Jesus into conversation?

God Awareness

1. How does child respond in conversation about God?

2. What statements does child make that reflect understanding of God?

3. What evidence does child give of awareness that God created the world?

Any significant indications of growth should be written down. Share your observations with parents to secure their insight about the child's behavior at home. Interaction between teacher and parent about the child's development can be very helpful for both.

Have You Tried These Ideas?

Parents' Observation of the Department ■ During the year, invite every parent to observe at least one session in their child's department. By seeing the department in action during a full session a parent can quickly understand the objectives and teaching methods of the department. Many parents have not seen their child interacting with a group of children. Observation in a group teaching situation can provide understanding of their own child.

The parents' presence may affect a child's behavior, but by careful handling this can be minimized. Talk with the parents ahead of time and ask them to come a little early. Provide seats away from the centers of activity. Ask them to avoid talking with teachers, children, or each other, as talking will distract the children. If a child initiates a conversation, the parents should respond briefly, then seek to guide the child back to the group. After the parents have observed a session, discuss their response and answer any questions they may have.

Open House ■ Plan a special open house for a Sunday afternoon, evening, weeknight or even as part of your regular session. The children may bring their parents and participate with them in learning activities used on Sunday morning. Even toddlers enjoy getting to "play with daddy" using the department's toys. Children may help make invitations and perhaps prepare some refreshments. Provide time for parents to ask questions about the department.

Parent-Teacher Meetings ■ These meetings are usually held in the evening and may include special speakers and films. Keep the emphasis on topics that will be helpful for the parents at home: discipline, activities to enjoy with your child, family worship with preschoolers, etc. Share a list of books useful for parents. A table with books available for borrowing or purchase is helpful for parents.

Mothers' Club ■ Many churches provide regular opportunities for young mothers to meet to discuss their concerns about their children. Resource people are usually provided to keep discussion productive. Often, there is a workshop format with mothers learning various home-craft skills. In many churches the Mother's Club is very informal and the group meets in homes. A Bible study or devotional period is usually included as part of the schedule.

Bulletin Boards and Monthly Bulletins ■ These may keep parents informed on many topics:

1. Unit goals and objectives
2. Special upcoming events and activities
3. Photographs of children and samples of their work
4. Activities in the church that would be of interest to parents
5. Recommended reading for parents *and* children
6. Photographs with personal information about teachers
7. A list of materials needed by the department which parents could possibly provide—for art and other activities, nature center, picture file, etc.
8. Help needed—in assistant teaching, making or repairing furniture, demonstrating a special activity.

Assistant Teaching ■ Once or twice a year, invite each parent to assist in teaching for a session or a unit. Many churches involve parents in this way during Churchtime, allowing them to work with a regular teacher. This not only gives the department added support, it gives parents opportunities to learn and practice new skills in teaching their own child. Contact the parents far enough ahead so they can schedule the time. Contact them again the week before to give instructions on what they will be doing and to share the Bible aims for that session. Parents assisting may help out at one activity center: books, puzzles and God's Wonders are usually the easiest places to begin. Or parents may demonstrate a special skill that would be of interest to the children. Working together in this way gives teachers an opportunity to build rapport with the parents.

Child Visit ■ Many teachers have found an excellent response to inviting one or two children home for Sunday afternoon. The children love it. The parents appreciate it, and the teacher finds it very effective in building closer relationships with each child. Many shy children have begun to open up at Sunday School following such a visit. Also, children who have been rebellious and defiant have made big strides in improved behavior. The advantages of inviting two at a time include: involving every child in your class more quickly, two can entertain each other, and good relationships are built between children.

YOUR COMMITMENT TO THE PARENTS

As you make personal contacts with parents, keep in mind the goal of establishing friendships and ministering spiritually to families. Become sensitive to needs they may have, including physical, material or social needs. Remember Jesus' teaching: "For I was hungry and you gave me something to eat, I was thirsty and you gave me something to drink, I was a stranger and you invited me in, I needed clothes and you clothed me, I was sick and you looked after me, I was in prison and you came to visit me . . . . 'I tell you the truth, whatever you did for one of the least of these brothers of mine, you did for me'" (Matt. 25:35,36,40). James also gives appropriate instruction: "Suppose a brother or sister is without clothes and daily food. If one of you says to him, 'Go, I wish you well; keep warm and well fed,' but does nothing about his physical needs, what good is it?" (Jas. 2:15,16).

You may be wondering how you are going to find time to become involved with six or seven families' lives. In order for you to have a ministry as effective as God wants it to be, teaching must be a priority in your use of time. Are there some areas in your schedule that should be dropped? Are you participating or serving in so many good causes that you cannot be truly effective in any? Make this a matter of prayerful thought to find ways of having a truly significant ministry.

Since the Bible strongly teaches that the home is the main center of teaching the Word, your ministry of helping families to become more Christ-centered should be as vital to you as planning the Sunday morning Bible story and learning activities.

God has given you a concern for young children. Ask Him to give you a concern for childrens' families both inside and outside the church. You have been called to minister to these homes in Jesus' name.

The Young Child's Approach to Learning

When three-year-old Matthew's father mentioned that they were expecting friends to drop by that evening, Matthew enthusiastically asked if he could meet them at the door. "I want to tell them where they live!"

"But, Matt, you don't know where they live," his father responded.

"That's why I want to *tell* them where they live," said Matthew, totally unaware that the word he should have used was "ask," not "tell." Matthew was too busy with all the excitement of living to worry about the definitions of words. After all, he knew what he meant.

Yet, he also is anxious to make his intentions clear to his father. Thus, over a period of time, as Matthew talks with Dad and Mom and teachers and friends, he corrects his errors and becomes more efficient in communicating.

We call this process learning.

Learning is what Matthew is doing most of his waking hours. He is learning as he plays, as he struggles to tie his shoes, as he mixes yellow into his blue finger painting, as he rides his tricycle, as he asks questions. From dawn to dark he never stops learning information, skills and attitudes. He is learning who he is, and how he relates to people and things, and yes, to God.

WHAT CAN YOUNG CHILDREN LEARN?

"I want my child to learn about God and the Bible and Jesus!"

Eric was two, and his mother was concerned that he learn. But where do you start with a young child? What is most important for Eric to learn about God? What is he ready to understand about the Bible? Which stories about Jesus will have the most meaning to him now?

The basic learning Eric needs for healthy development must involve not only knowledge about facts, but attitudes and behavior as well. Most teachers and parents tend to approach instruction for the child assuming that knowledge will produce appropriate feelings which will result in proper actions. This may be true for some adult learning experiences, but it is really backwards from the way young children learn.

The young child must first experience something (using as many of the five senses as possible). From each experience grow feelings and understandings—and rarely in a neat, logical fashion. The following paragraphs consider six major areas in which young children need guidance. However, while it is helpful to identify areas of the child's learning, the child is never learning in neat categories. The young child's insatiable curiosity is constantly processing experiences, feelings and understandings in ways that frequently leave adults wondering, "How did she ever learn that?"

Self

Every child looks at the world from the inside out. All the external contacts of life are viewed through the filter of the child's inner feelings and understandings. Thus, a child's self-perception is a crucial factor in the child's response to everyone else, to every experience of life, and ultimately to God. The self-concept which each child develops is fragile; it can be lovingly nourished into a healthy and positive outlook, or it can be damaged by neglect and by abuse.

The young child needs opportunities to **experience:**
- making suitable choices;
- meeting new situations;
- displaying appropriate independence and dependence;
- talking with teachers and friends;
- working successfully at tasks;

- facing and overcoming difficulties;
- repeating enjoyable activities.

These experiences need to be planned to elicit **feelings** of love and security and gratitude, such as:
- receiving and giving affection both verbally and physically;
- expressing feelings openly;
- receiving specific praise and encouragement for who the child is and for what the child does.

Every young child needs someone to add conversation to these experiences so that the child may **know:**
- "You are special because God made you and loves you."
- "You are growing and learning as God planned."
- "You can do many good things."
- "You are important to God and to me."

Others

The young child learns about other people at the same time perceptions about self are growing. Reactions to family members, friends, teachers and other people color, and are colored by, the child's view of self. The child begins to love others in the way love has been experienced. Respect for others parallels the respect the child has received. The child's view of others is a mirror image of how the child sees him or herself.

Every child needs to **experience:**
- positive personal interaction with parents, teachers and peers;
- participating in group activities;
- respecting the rights of others;
- taking turns, helping and sharing.

These experiences contribute to **feelings** of:
- acceptance by family and friends;
- love toward specific people;
- interest in and respect for others;

- enjoyment of interaction with others;
- desire to help others.

Appropriate conversation should accompany these experiences to help build the child's **knowledge**. For example:
- "God made and loves everyone."
- "God planned for people (family, teachers, friends, etc.) to love and care for you."
- "God wants us to love and be kind to others."

Church

The term "church" is often used by people to denote a building. Not only is that use inaccurate (the Bible uses "church" to refer to people), it can create some unfortunate concepts in a child's thinking. For example, a child who had been taught that the "church" was "God's house," was fearful that God could not hear her bedtime prayers because He was across town at His "house."

Young children need a variety of **experiences** when they come together with other church people:
- listening, praying, singing;
- sharing, helping and giving;
- working and playing cooperatively with others;
- caring for the church's building, equipment and materials;
- observing teachers as models of Christian attitudes and actions;
- going to teachers for help and information.

Positive **feelings** should be nurtured through these experiences:
- love and acceptance by church people;
- security, comfort and happiness in church activities;
- desire to be with others in church.

Help the child **know**:
- "The church is people, all kinds of people, who love Jesus."
- "We like to come together to learn about God and Jesus."

- "We sing and pray because we love God."
- "Our room is planned to help us learn and play together."

Bible and Prayer

The Bible and prayer are the means of communication between God and us, and they both have a mysterious attraction for young children. While there is much about both that the young child cannot comprehend, there are some highly meaningful experiences and concepts which are of great benefit in the early years of a child's life.

The child needs **experiences** of:
- listening to and talking about appropriate Bible stories (the best Bible stories for a young child are those with an obvious, literal connection to the child's experience);
- imitating the good examples of Bible characters;
- listening to others pray;
- talking to God in a variety of situations.

Some of the positive **feelings** which grow from such pleasant experiences include:
- a desire to hear Bible stories;
- confidence in the goodness of Bible commands;
- willingness to talk to God about items of concern;
- assurance that God hears the child's prayers.

The child's **knowledge** about the Bible and prayer will grow through helpful conversation, such as:
- "The Bible is a special book about God and Jesus."
- "The stories in the Bible are true."
- "The Bible helps us know good things to do."
- "You can talk to God at any time about anything."
- "God listens when you pray."

Jesus

The young child is easily attracted to Jesus. Jesus is such a warm, sympathetic person who obviously likes children, that children readily like Him. These early perceptions form the foundation for the child receiving Christ as Savior and desiring to follow His example in godly living. While some children in this age level may pray to become a member of God's family, accepting Jesus as Savior, expect wide variations in children's readiness for this important step.

Experiences which help the child learn about Jesus include:
- listening to and talking about stories of Jesus;
- singing songs about Jesus;
- observing teachers' examples of Christlike behavior;
- imitating Jesus' example in specific situations;
- praying for God's help to become more like Jesus.

Expect the child to **feel**:
- love for Jesus;
- gratitude for His kindness;
- desire to do good things as Jesus did;
- concern for having knowingly done wrong things.

Some of the things a child needs to **know** are:
- "Jesus was born as a baby, grew to be a child, and then became a grown-up man."
- "Jesus did kind, loving things."
- "Jesus taught people about God."
- "Jesus was God's special Son, and came to show God's love to everyone."
- "Jesus let people kill Him. He died to take the punishment for the wrong things we have done."
- "Jesus rose from the dead. That means He's not dead anymore. He is still alive."
- "Jesus loves you."

God

Not being able to touch God or even see pictures of Him, the child's learning of God is totally dependent on what people say and show about God. In a very real sense, parents and teachers are like God to the child. As you demonstrate and talk about God's love, the child begins to formulate some concrete impressions of who God is. Expect the young child to cast all ideas of God in literal, physical terms. The spiritual, transcendent nature of God is beyond the young child's level of mental development.

Help the child **experience** God's presence in our world through:
- seeing, touching, smelling, tasting and hearing things God has made;
- talking and singing about God;
- hearing stories of God's involvement with people;
- praying spontaneously in the midst of situations of interest to the child;
- naming ways God has planned to care for us;
- thanking God for His goodness;
- obeying God's commands.

A growing awareness of God results in **feelings** of:
- gratitude and joy for God's love and care;
- awe at God's great power and knowledge;
- desire to please God by doing good things;

Build the child's **knowledge** of God by talking naturally about Him and things He has done:
- "God made all things."
- "God is love."
- "God is good."
- "God cares for you."
- "God knows what is good for us to do."
- "God forgives us when we tell Him we have done something wrong."

Most efforts to teach young children focus on the things adults want children to *know*. While accurate information is important and is expressed through words, words and facts are very imperfect vehicles for the learning child. In order for knowledge to have a significant impact on the kind of person a child is becoming, words must be combined with experience in a way that produces positive attitudes. If you want to see long-term results for your efforts, you must give considerable attention to all dimensions of a child's learning, not merely transmitting truth, but demonstrating it in practical ways.

HOW DO YOUNG CHILDREN LEARN?

How do you learn? How do you acquire information or develop opinions? Perhaps by reading books? By listening to a lecture or sermon, by watching a film or television program? By discussion with someone else? Much adult learning is by means of *words*, symbols by which we are able to communicate.

Learning in early childhood is different from learning as an adult, however. The mind of the child is not capable of handling ideas coming in words only. The young child does not have the ability to give real meaning to a "flat" word unless it is a very familiar part of experience and evokes ideas and feelings from memory.

Through the Senses

While we cannot know all that occurs in the mind of a young child, we do know that information enters the mind through the gates of the senses—seeing, feeling, smelling, tasting and hearing.

Firsthand experiences are the hard core of learning for young children. Efforts to produce learning must involve as many of the child's five senses as possible.

When two-year-old Hannah pleaded, "Let me see it!" she really meant, "Let me feel it, touch it, shake it, put it in my mouth, rub it against my cheek and take a deep breath to see how it smells!" Through the senses the child learns of God's world and the people in it.

For example, eating an apple is a very satisfactory sensory

experience. God made apples in a way that appeals to all of the senses. They are bright red or green, or else their color is delicately shaded. Their shape is round, fitting securely into the hand. The firmness of the fruit makes touching them a joy. They can be rolled around in the hand. Their aroma causes digestive juices to run. Their taste is delicate but distinctive, and their crunch as one bites into them is unmistakable. Eating an apple is a total sensory experience which is unforgettable to the child and will enrich the child's memories for the rest of his or her life.

Try offering a child a piece of apple to taste. Wait for a smile at the flavor, then ask, "Would you like to thank God for apples?" The resulting one-sentence prayer will be spoken with genuine thanksgiving.

By Repetition

The activities you offer need not change every week. In fact, they *should* not. A child who feels happy and satisfied with a learning experience will want to repeat it. Repetition is a necessary (and natural) part of a child's learning. Songs and stories become favorites only when they are enjoyed over and over.

While Kyle and Erica were building with blocks, Miss Lee began to sing, "Who made Kyle's hands? Who made Erica's hands? God made Kyle's hands and God made Erica's hands." Later, during Together Time, the whole department sang, "Who made my hands?" Throughout the morning the song was sung during various activities. On the way home, Kyle grandly announced, "I know a song about Kyle's hands!"

By Many Varied Experiences

Children need new experiences as well as opportunities to repeat their learning in different ways. For example, a child learning to be kind, helpful and loving needs many different experiences where those words are attached to specific actions, including those of teachers and friends.

While the Good Samaritan story is an action-packed narrative, a story is not the best way to begin teaching a child to be kind. The impact of a story is greatest when it is told after children have had opportunity to practice the behavior mentioned.

The Sunday Mrs. Evers told the Good Samaritan story, she had the children make Get Well cards at the art table to practice an act of kindness. At the same time, Mr. Tucker was showing some other children how to be kind to the guinea pig in the God's Wonders center. Mrs. Avila was acting out a visit to the doctor with some of the children in the Home Living corner, enabling them to see the doctor as a kind helper who cares for them. Later, when Mr. Tucker told the Bible story, he reminded them of ways he had seen them help that morning, "just like the kind man in our story."

By Practice in Play

The child also needs opportunities to practice through firsthand play experiences that can be repeated in everyday life. Repetition through play strengthens habits, attitudes, knowledge and understanding that reflect Christian values. For this reason, plan learning activities which incorporate such skills as problem solving, getting along with other children, listening and speaking, and role-playing. Conversation using Bible verses should be a part of the activities. Children learn because they are *doing*. And for young children, doing is play.

Play does not sound very educational—or spiritual. But play is a child's full-time occupation: it is the activity through which the child learns best. Adults often distinguish between work and play. Not so with young children! For the young child the time given to play is just as significant, demanding and exhausting as the time adults spend at work or in managing the home. Blocks, dolls, puzzles and paints are the tools children use in play. They are tools by which children can learn Bible truth when properly guided by alert teachers.

By Imitation

"Born to Mimic" is a label every child wears. From infancy the child continually picks up ways of doing things from observation of others. Thus, your role among young children is not just to do "teacher things," but to participate with children in the midst of their activity. Your role is not so much to direct children in what they are to do, but to participate with them. If you make a point to carefully put puzzles away, children will learn to care for materials. If you smile while pulling apart some play dough, children will join in with pleasure. If you bow your head to thank God for the alfalfa seeds the children planted, they will learn to pray in the midst of daily activities.

By Connecting Words to Actions

Words are the building blocks of thoughts. We must have words to define the concepts we use in thinking. Children have limited vocabularies and experience. This combination results in a limited ability to manipulate concepts. When you take a bite of an apple, you may think, "That tastes good! I'm glad God made apples!" The young child, however, may only think, "Mmm!" You must provide words, helping the child to respond to the experience and relating God to the event. Once this relationship is made, the child is able to think about God the next time something tastes good. Without your words, the experience would be simply another of many taste sensations to be stored for later reference.

WHAT FACTORS AFFECT
THE YOUNG CHILD'S LEARNING?

Past Experience

The information entering by the gateway of the senses is processed by each child's mind in uniquely individual ways. All the child's experiences, at home, at church, at school, are the basis for assimilating the information you are trying to communicate.

Bryan has been successful in the past at cutting, so he may choose that activity eagerly. He will listen to your directions, relate your words to previous encounters with scissors and be eager to get to work. He will be able to talk with you about the pictures he is cutting. However, Sara has had difficulty with scissors in the past and may come with some reluctance. She may not be capable of focusing on following your directions. She may not respond at all to conversation about the pictures because she is too busy concentrating on cutting to hear what you say.

Experiences shape attitudes and expectations. An alert teacher can help a child build positive attitudes by working with the child to insure success. Sara's teacher quickly saw her difficulty. "Sara, I'll hold the paper while you cut it." At each laborious stroke of the scissors, the teacher praised Sara's effort. No mention was made of missing the line. The important thing was that Sara was cutting! Gradually, Sara's attitude changed from defeat and frustration to positive confidence that she could cut. This was due to the teacher giving just enough help so that Sara could succeed, then praising her efforts. Sara's estimate of her success will be the basis for a positive attitude in later experiences.

A Self-centered Viewpoint

The young child's thinking automatically focuses on self rather than others. The child assumes that everybody else views things exactly as he or she does. Two-year-old Michelle dramatically demonstrated this quality when she attempted to hide herself during a game of hide-and-seek by crouching in the middle of the floor and tightly closing her eyes. Her assumption was that if she could not see others, they could not see her!

Three-year-old Brandon, who stood up to get a better look, was not concerned that children behind him then could not see at all. This self-centered approach to the world is often annoying, but normal at this stage. The child needs adults to give gentle guidance in dealing with the inevitable conflicts caused by this limited viewpoint.

The child needs many opportunities to interact with others in order to begin recognizing other points of view. Imaginative play is one of the best devices the child has for this learning. When

Rachel was playing "mother," her dealings with her "children" helped her consider how her own mother thinks and feels.

Concrete Interpretations

Because the child learns through physical experiences with people and things, all thinking focuses on that which is concrete and tangible. Symbolism and abstractions that convey great meaning to adults usually communicate little to a child. Sometimes a child's literal view of life creates comic results, as with six-year-old Katie who announced that Jesus got into her heart by "sliding down my tongue." Deeper thought about her remark removed the humor, however, when teachers realized that the practice of referring to "Jesus in my heart" had led her to visualize only a tiny figure of a man sitting somewhere inside her chest.

Implications of These Factors

It is important to understand these factors that influence a child's thinking, so that materials and methods can be appropriately chosen to accomplish meaningful learning.

Because the young child interprets experiences on the basis of past success or failure:
- provide a wide variety of activities in which the child can succeed.

Because the young child views the world from a self-centered perspective:
- structure opportunities for interaction with others and for imaginative play.

Because the young child interprets information concretely:
- carefully avoid symbolism and abstractions as you present information.

WHAT NEEDS AFFECT LEARNING?

While every child has specific, personal needs, there are also basic needs which are common to all children. Both types of needs influence the child's learning.

Physical Needs

These are usually fairly obvious and include such needs as physi-. cal activity, rest, food, water and touch. Until the physical needs are met, the child is not able to give energy and attention to learning. Subsequent chapters deal in greater detail with many of these needs at specific age levels.

Safety and Security

It is also obvious that children need to be protected from *physical harm*. To prevent accidents, be alert for potentially danger-ous situations. Check toys and other equipment regularly for sharp points and edges. Be sure furniture is sturdy, free from splinters and sharp corners.

Be alert for the child who does not feel well. Help parents be aware of the need for enforcing sensible health and safety regu-lations to protect all the children. A child who is ill should always be kept at home.

We must also protect children from *emotional harm*. Accept their emotional needs and be ready to help meet them. Fear, anger, loneliness and frustration are common emotions for which children need understanding adults to help them cope. Never ridicule or shame them. Help them feel secure in your love and protection.

The child finds security in familiar people, surroundings and procedures. Be consistent in your attendance so children learn to depend on you. Plan a program that follows the same general routine every session. Supply basic equipment that will be avail-able to the child every Sunday, allowing the child to enjoy using the same materials again and again. Repeat Bible stories and sing familiar songs throughout each week of a unit.

The young child also finds security in limits. The child needs to know what is expected, what can and cannot be done. Estab-lishing limits to insure children's physical safety is your first con-sideration. (For instance, no child may leave the room alone.) Also set limits for the appropriate use of equipment and materials. For example, puzzle pieces must be kept on the table; blocks remain in the building area; Home Living equipment must not be stepped on. Allow as much freedom as possible within these limits, but be consistent. The same limits should apply during Sunday School, Churchtime and any other occasion when the room is used. When you remind a child of the limits, it helps to phrase your words positively. "We need to keep puzzle pieces on the table," rather than, "Don't carry away the puzzle pieces."

Love and Acceptance

Feeling loved is essential to a child's well being. The Lord said, "I have loved you with an everlasting love" (Jer. 31:3). All people need love that is unconditional and ever available. Christ offers this to us and we must express it to the child. Love that does not depend on circumstances or behavior offers a child opportunity for growth and development in all areas of his or her life.

Your helpful actions, your smile, even your tone of voice can say, "I love you." For one child a smile across the room or a friendly pat on the shoulder is enough to let her know you care. For another it takes a hug or a few minutes of cuddling to communicate concern for him.

Usually, the child who seems the least lovable is the one who needs love the most. Pray for that child and ask God to show love through you. Every child needs to feel loved and accepted regardless of what he or she does or does not do.

Acceptance is not the same thing as approval. Acceptance simply means acknowledging a child's feelings. When a child exhibits feelings of anger or unfriendliness, accept the child even though you do not approve of the child's actions.

In order to accept a child, you must be aware of the child as a unique person. How well do you know each child in your class? Observe each one thoughtfully; and listen to their chatter as they play. Arrange to meet the parents, asking them for suggestions on ways to meet their child's interests and needs. Learning to understand each child will provide a sound basis for loving acceptance.

Esteem

Recognition of the child's worth goes hand-in-hand with providing love and acceptance. Consider how Jesus demonstrated children's importance to Him when He interrupted an adult discussion to hold small children on His lap. Jesus clearly affirmed the dignity and value of the young child. He saw little ones possessing unique qualities and personal worth.

To nurture healthy esteem in the child:
- Be realistic and consistent in your expectations of what the child can do;
- Be loving and firm when correction is needed;
- Extend common courtesies you would show an adult friend (i.e., "please," "thank you," "excuse me," "I'm sorry," etc.);
- Give the child a few minutes notice before ending an enjoyable activity;
- Avoid shaming or labeling a child;
- Avoid talking about a child when the child is present.

Development of Personal Potential

Every child needs to develop his or her potential in every area—physical skills, intellectual understanding, social interaction, emotional expression and spiritual insight. Your responsibility is to help each child develop, at his or her own rate, to become all God intends in every area of life.

A child is not born with the ability to control actions or emotions. The child must develop self-control with the careful guidance of trusted adults. Developing this self-control does not happen overnight. It takes time. A child first needs to know what adults expect. After these limits have been tested and found to be consistent, the child can begin to develop self-control. By adhering to a well-organized routine and enforcing a few rules of conduct, adults encourage the child to be responsible, to practice discipline from within.

The young child's, "Let me do it!" is evidence of the first steps toward self-control and independence. The child is attempting to discover his or her own abilities. While the child needs to do things independently, there is also a high need for assurance that an understanding teacher is nearby if assistance is needed.

Careful, thoughtful guidance is needed to help the child develop competence in a world built for people more than twice the child's size. Your role is to give the child freedom in choosing from among the materials and activities available. For example, arrange materials so the child knows where they are, can reach them without asking for assistance and return them when finished.

Give the child as much independence as possible. Encourage the child's efforts and praise any accomplishments. When it is necessary to assist, give suggestions that will enable the child to experience success, not just sit and watch you complete the activity.

For example, "Do you think the puzzle piece will fit if you turn it around?" or "It might be easier for you to hang up your coat if I hold the hanger very still." As the child experiences success in using rapidly developing skills, confidence grows and the child is encouraged to attempt more challenging endeavors.

As we meet these basic needs of the child, we make it possible for learning to take place. The child becomes able to concentrate on the new experiences and information we offer.

HOW DO "SPECIAL" CHILDREN LEARN?

Every child is a unique miracle of God's making. From before the time of birth each one is different from all others—God planned it so.

Most teachers prepare for the "average" child. Since almost every child is outside the "average" range in some area of development, there is great need for teachers to be flexible in lesson planning. This need is intensified whenever there is a child in the group who is significantly different from most of the other children.

Expect young children to respond in many different ways to

any given activity. For example, one teacher prepared an activity for children to glue magazine pictures of people God made. One boy was only interested in the gluing, taking whatever picture was on top of the pile and laboriously adding it to his page which became covered with pictures. Next to him were two girls who took great pains to find particular kinds of people. Across the table was a boy who wanted to write the "names" below his pictures. And then there was a girl who quickly glued two pictures, announced she was done, and hurried over to the Home Living area! All were happy with what they were doing, for they were encouraged to work at their own level.

Joshua was a gifted child who often caused a disturbance in the room. His teachers began giving Joshua extra personal attention. They discussed ways each activity could be stretched to make it more challenging for him. He was made responsible for jobs and was given recognition for his positive actions. Eventually, Joshua could participate happily, for his unique needs were being met. Instead of trying to pressure Joshua into doing everything the same as others, his teachers challenged him, making him feel accepted within the Christian community.

Kim was a little girl who was a slow learner. Physically she was developing normally, but she was not as quick to grasp new ideas as her peers. Her Sunday School teachers made a commitment to provide normal learning experiences at her own pace for Kim. For example, her attention span was very short. When she lost interest in the Bible story, the department leader would invite her to look at a book—and would provide her the same learning as the other children received, except on a personal basis. She was thus able to grow without being deprived of those early learning experiences which are so important for mental development. Had Kim simply been "left out" because she was unable to keep up with others her age, her likelihood of normal development would have been much more limited. Today Kim is still a slow learner, but she has become a good group member and is loved by all those she is around. Her abilities also seem to be increasing beyond what was expected.

It is important that we remember that every person in the Body of Christ is important and significant. Intelligence and abilities are not God's standard for assessing spirituality. God does not ask us our IQ. His measure is love.

The Baby and the Toddler

I knew I had made a difference. While there have been many Sunday mornings I have wondered whether anyone would have missed me if I had stayed in bed, this was not one of them. I knew without any doubt that my being there that day had made a difference.

Jennifer was eleven months old and she did not want her mom to leave her in my Sunday School room. People in the next building knew that Jennifer did not want her mom to leave her. I'm not a big advocate of trying to strip toddlers away from their mothers so they'll learn to be independent. I tend to have a lot of respect for a child's God-given need for security. But Jennifer's mom was calling the shots and she felt she needed to leave. I took Jennifer in my arms and she proceeded to plant her feet firmly in my midsection, either in an effort to generate leverage for a planned escape or to give her a solid foundation for her continuing vocal protests.

As with most separation battles, Jennifer calmed down a few minutes after her mom left, and I began to think this was going to be a fairly quiet morning after all. Then I started to put her down. As reluctantly as she had come to me to begin with, she had now decided I was definitely worth hanging onto. When three other toddlers with quivering lower lips looked wistfully our way, I decided a few more minutes of holding her might be a wise thing to do.

Those few minutes stretched and my arms ached as Jennifer

and I remained glued together, walking back and forth across the toy-strewn floor. We looked out the window together as I described the color, make and model of every car in the parking lot. We examined the flower pattern in the wallpaper. We (meaning I) picked up a wide variety of enchanting toys and dropped (meaning she) them immediately back onto the floor. I sweetly sang every lullaby I knew and recited with feeling the 23rd Psalm, the Gettysburg Address and the Preamble to the Constitution.

We returned repeatedly to the bulletin board and gazed at an appealing picture of Jesus holding some adorable children (none of whom was clinging as desperately as Jennifer). I sang wonderfully inventive songs about Jesus and Jennifer and began to wonder if my blood was able to circulate past the stranglehold she had applied to my neck.

And then Jennifer's mother returned. Awkwardly I handed Jennifer across the counter and mumbled something about no more tears. Mom seemed grateful that the screaming had stopped and told me she had slipped out of church twice to listen outside our door. As mom retreated out the door with diaper bag in one arm and Jennifer in the other, Jennifer looked back at me. Then she waved. And she smiled. That was when I knew I had made a difference. As I stood on the steps outside the church and gently massaged my blood back into motion, I said, "Thanks, Lord, for letting me be where someone really needed me."

THE CHILD FROM BIRTH TO SIX MONTHS

Physical Development

Observe a child through the first six months of life. You will see a change from a little bundle which makes only reflexive grasping motions and sleeps nearly 20 hours a day, to a baby who is able to lift head and probably chest off the mattress, sit up with support, grab purposefully at hanging toys and perhaps hold onto a bottle.

Most children up to the age of six months will remain in one place, although by the end of that period some are becoming mobile. Physical development during this period is tremendous but the baby continues to be extremely dependent. The infant must rely on someone else to take care of all physical comfort needs from feeding, to changing, to turning over in the crib.

Facilities and Equipment

Facilities for baby care at church must accommodate all of the young child's needs. Infants need a place where they are safe from the probing fingers of older babies and toddlers, preferably in a room of their own with equipment designed for their age. (See chapter 9 for details.)

Social Development

A baby is more responsive to people than to anything else in the environment. A newborn quickly establishes eye contact. Smiles become common around two months. Always, baby is sensitive to the moods of those nearby.

Always gently approach the baby, making soft, soothing sounds. Hold the baby; talk softly and make the baby comfortable. The baby needs to feel safe, warm and loved. Consistently reflect God's love as you feed and change the baby. Show the child you are glad to do this. Even infants are quick to sense any displeasure you have in burping them or changing their diapers.

Ask parents for the baby's feeding schedule in writing. Then follow it exactly. Feed, burp and rock baby without rushing. Humming and soft singing help you and baby stay relaxed.

The attitude in which a baby's needs are met now will greatly influence his or her developing personality and approach to the world. For instance, the child whose needs are quickly and lovingly met begins to feel able to affect the environment. A consistent pattern of warm attention will encourage a baby to trust people and have a confident approach to life. Children who are ignored and left to cry for long periods have been observed to become less and less communicative, as if they realize that efforts at communication are useless.

Sing-song rhymes and simple songs are a natural kind of conversation with babies. Singing and humming provide sooth-ing sounds that contribute to a peaceful atmosphere. Babies soon begin to respond to favorites, such as "Jesus Loves Me," "God Cares for You" and "Bye-Low, My Baby,"[1] when they hear them over and over again.

During these first months the baby develops a social person-ality and grows to know a regular nursery teacher. The baby learns to relax when friendly, loving hands provide support and cuddling. This makes it important that a staff of regular workers be maintained so that the little ones can begin to identify with their "friend at church."

Crying

All babies cry, but there are great variations from baby to baby. Some babies cry more readily and more intensely than others. When a baby cries hard the legs are pulled up and every muscle tightened. The face turns red and the arms wave about. Crying is the only way the baby can tell you about discomfort or fear.

As you care for a baby on a regular basis you learn to distin-guish one cry from another. There is usually a difference in tone and pitch between the hunger cry, the fretting cry, and the cry of pain or discomfort. Careful observation as a nursery teacher will help you to gain this awareness.

Regardless of your ability to distinguish cries, make sure your assumptions are right by investigating thoroughly. Try burping the baby in case gas is causing discomfort. Or, if the mother has sent a bottle, check whether the baby is hungry by offering the bottle. Perhaps the problem is a wet or soiled diaper; investigate and change diapers if necessary.

Make sure you have some sort of system for checking dia-pers. A mimeographed attendance chart to which names can be added each Sunday can be checked as you change each baby. This will help you see that resting babies are also checked for wet or soiled diapers during the occasional quiet moments.

Once you have done everything you can to make the baby comfortable, yet crying continues, the baby may need to be held and comforted. It is unlikely you will "spoil" a baby by holding him or her during the one or two hours a week in the nursery.

Remember, your calm and gentle voice helps babies feel reassured long before they understand your words. Avoid baby-talk. Use short simple sentences with words that mean exactly what they say. "I love Maria. God loves Maria." As the teacher cuddles Maria and smiles warmly, Maria begins to associate the word "God" with a pleasant experience.

Security-seeking Behaviors

Other behaviors which cause teachers some anxiety are those which the child uses to gain security, (i.e., thumb-sucking, blanket carrying, and banging or rocking). Each of these behaviors is perfectly normal in the infant. These behaviors manifest themselves frequently under stress or tension or before the baby goes to sleep. Therefore, the teacher's calm acceptance of the child in the face of these behaviors will go a long way toward helping the child to overcome them.

Studies have shown that many healthy babies enjoy sucking their thumbs even though they are not fatigued, hungry or uncomfortable. Thumb-sucking in most babies ceases eventually if undue attention is not paid to it.

Blanket carrying is another behavior that infants and young children exhibit frequently. For some reason, the child derives great comfort and security from holding an old rag or a particular soft toy and doesn't want to part with it for even a few hours. The baby may tuck it under one arm and constantly rub it between two fingers or hold it during thumb-sucking. This, too, will eventually be given up as the child matures.

Some babies bump their heads against the crib or rock from side to side instead of sucking their thumbs. This is the same type of rhythmic activity as thumb-sucking. Even though you may think the baby is hitting very hard, it is unlikely damage will result, but you may provide cribs with four-sided bumper pads to soften the blows.

Intellectual Growth

Learning begins the minute the baby begins to record observations about the environment. This may well occur before birth.

You can aid in this development by providing stimuli for the baby's senses. A baby who cries for no apparent reason may simply be bored and will respond positively to colorful things to see and new sounds to hear. A crib mobile will provide something interesting to look at while in the lying and watching stage. When baby begins to reach for things and tries to grasp them, it is time to place one or two bright toys within reach. A small rattle or a brightly-colored fabric doll which is easily held will be just right. (All toys should be washable and should be sterilized after every session.) Hang toys by strings from a piece of elastic stretched across the crib or playpen. This will save you steps and the baby will learn to grab the toys. The elastic will help the toys move or react to the baby's move to pull the toys close.

Babies quickly develop the knack of putting everything they find into their mouths. This is an essential part of their learning but can also be dangerous. Check the floor carefully on Sunday morning before the infants arrive and pick up any items that may have been dropped. Small buttons or pins may not be easily noticed but will be found by the infant who is becoming mobile.

Milestones of Development

Listed next are some behaviors you may observe in the infant from birth to six months. Each child is unique and will follow this pattern at a unique rate and may skip some behaviors or not develop them until later.

By three months the baby may:
- hold the head well off the bed when placed on his or her abdomen;
- smile in response to your voice;

- use eyes to follow a moving person or object;
- stare at a bright object;
- turn head to voice or familiar sound.

Between three and four months the baby may:
- begin to grasp a toy;
- push up using the arms;
- coo and gurgle with pleasure;
- roll from back to side;
- be quieted by a voice or by music;
- begin to play with hands;
- turn the head freely to watch activities and objects;
- smile and respond to friendly overtures;
- hold the head erect;
- vocalize, cough or click the tongue to initiate "conversation."

Between four and six months the baby may:
- laugh out loud;
- hold onto toys;
- wave hands in order to be lifted;
- reach for objects;
- make noise upon hearing a voice;
- lift head and shoulders and roll over;
- roll from back to stomach;
- sit up with some propping.

THE CHILD FROM SIX MONTHS TO EIGHTEEN MONTHS

Physical Development

During the child's second half year, changes come almost faster than we can chart them. The ability to move around increases almost daily. Baby crawls actively and sits upright for a period of time. The first teeth begin to come in and solid food is added to the diet. The baby explores the world by mouth, biting and tasting everything within reach. The child grabs a toy in the crib, drops it, bangs a fist in protest, cries and then repeats the sequence all over again. After learning to pinch thumb and forefinger together, the child tries to hold a bottle and drink.

The ability to spend time "sitting up" means the baby is ready for a whole series of new experiences. Both hands are free to manipulate toys and to hold books and pictures for close inspection. Often you will notice that a baby's hands and feet are the favorite toys and are always available.

The baby who is creeping soon pulls up on furniture and stands alone. The child exerts independence by crawling away, resisting dressing, refusing a bottle, kicking and screaming. As the child nears the first birthday, holding onto furniture provides support for walking until balance and strength combine in the first independent step.

After gaining confidence in standing ability, the child will begin to take a few tentative steps, still holding on to the furniture or playpen rail. Let the child set the pace, and somewhere between the twelfth and fifteenth month walking will begin.

Once a child has left the crib for crawling or walking experiences, safety measures are a vital consideration. Check equipment for sharp edges, loose pieces, cleanliness, chipping paint or any other potential safety hazard. Also check doors, windows or any openings through which a child might venture. Equip electric outlets with safety covers.

Facilities and Equipment

The room should be equipped with a few cribs for those babies who will need to nap. Because older babies want to move about, provide ample floor space. (See chapter 9 for details.)

Mental and Emotional Development

At about six months the infant often quite suddenly becomes shy and afraid of strangers. A child who has previously been quite happy in the church nursery may now begin to cry when mother leaves. A newborn cannot differentiate between all the varied people and components in the surrounding world. Slowly the baby begins to distinguish the familiar from the unfamiliar. Crying at this point is definitely a step of progress.

Sometime during this year, a baby discovers the ability to make decisions. One evidence of this growth occurs when the child resists your efforts to get him or her to do things. The child also becomes more and more energetic and, in the urge to explore, will be "into everything."

Babies want to touch and handle everything they see. Sometimes, for their own safety, you will have to hold them back. Avoid unnecessarily limiting this growing desire to explore, however, since investigation is the best way children have to learn about the world about them. When an interesting activity must be curtailed, a child may feel frustrated and then become angry. Quickly provide a substitute activity to help the child continue to explore in a positive and safe manner.

Play

Play occupies an increasingly large place in the child's life. A child plays spontaneously. You don't have to teach a baby how to play or even provide special toys. The urge comes from within, and the child will play with whatever is at hand.

A child learns, develops and builds knowledge through play. Most of a child's play is alone or with an adult. The baby enjoys peek-a-boo and a favorite of toddlers is hide-and-seek, as long as the child or the hidden object can be found quickly.

As a child begins to explore the world by creeping and walking, the companionship of youngsters somewhere near his or her own age becomes increasingly enjoyable.

At this stage children will not play cooperatively. They will show an interest in each other, but they will play with their own toys for short periods of time. There will be few squabbles because they are too absorbed in their own play to worry about what a companion may be doing.

Select those toys which will allow a child to express creativity and imagination. A child this age will enjoy large, colorful toys with movable parts which are easy to manipulate. The crawler will enjoy putting things together, such as placing one empty box in another, or fitting pans inside other pans. Fitting pegs or various shapes into their proper holes on a board is another favorite.

The toys should be stored in a toy cupboard or on shelves low enough for the children to reach, rather than in a bin where they become jumbled and often broken.

Verbal Activity

The child enjoys hearing simple conversation and songs. Soon the child begins to imitate sounds and learns to distinguish the tone of voice of the people nearby.

Around the time of the first birthday, most children will say their first word. Sometimes this first word will go completely unnoticed for a while simply because it doesn't sound like the word the baby is trying to imitate. But after using a certain sound several times to indicate a certain thing, adults catch on to the intended meaning.

Many babies will not "perform" for strangers and so, although they may be using a few words at home, they will probably not use them in the nursery at first.

The baby may stop adding new words for a while after the first two or three are understood. There may be a halt, too, while learning to walk, but the child will quickly make up for lost time. In the meantime, continue talking to the child using short, simple words. Sing nursery songs and recite rhymes. A few very simple finger plays and sentences can be introduced at this stage also. Do not talk too fast, though, and keep sentences short and simple.

Encourage children in their efforts to talk. Avoid the temptation to mimic baby talk. Babies learn by imitating the way adults talk. If you reverse the procedure and adopt their way of saying things, they will not be given the opportunity to learn the right way. Do not try to make children change the way they pronounce words, however. Just say the words they use clearly and correctly each time you use them. Also, respond to baby's babbling with clear statements. For instance, a child struggling to pull a teddy bear through the bars of a playpen may be frustratedly saying, "Dah-dah! Dah-dah!" As you help out, say, "Here's the teddy bear."

Milestones of Development

Having discussed infant stages from 6 to 18 months, the following lists may help you as you observe the babies you are teaching in the nursery.

Between the ages of six and eight months the baby may:
- object noisily when an object is taken away;
- recover a rattle if it falls within easy reach;
- reach for paper;
- cough artificially and enjoy being "cute";
- discriminate between a stranger and a familiar person.

Between the ages of 8 and 12 months the baby may:
- sit up well without support;
- bang spoon or pat table in play;
- be more active with a little help;
- pick up a cube or block off the table;
- hold a block in each hand;
- show temper if frustrated or thwarted;
- show pleasure by cooing or crowing.

Between the ages of 12 and 18 months the baby may:
- walk alone or with a little help;
- lower body from a standing to sitting position;
- repeat actions if laughed at;
- blow bubbles;
- hold a cup to drink from;
- stop when spoken to;
- show a little cooperation in helping to get dressed;
- build a tower of two or more blocks and fit a peg into its proper hole in a board;
- have a 5- to 10-word vocabulary.

THE CHILD FROM EIGHTEEN MONTHS TO TWO YEARS (TODDLERS)

Physical Development

Walking brings many changes to the child and everyone nearby. From now on life is a compromise between the toddler's fierce desire to be in control and the adult's good sense. Activities at church must be well planned, for the growing child has many interests, insatiable curiosity and no sense of danger. The environment must be safe for exploring. (See chapter 9 for information on facilities.)

A toddler has a tremendous urge to be independent. The toddler walks, climbs, falls, takes off clothing, handles finger food and invades the activities of other children. This rapidly growing ability to use all body parts dominates the child's attention and energy.

No matter how hard a toddler tries, or how earnestly you encourage, the child cannot exercise much deliberate control over feelings or behavior. The child needs space in which to move and practice movements which gradually become more relaxed and more controlled. Soft, flexible toys are excellent for channeling motor activity and cannot hurt the young child.

Physical play, even gentle roughhousing on the floor, is endlessly satisfying to the toddler who loves to be noisily followed— and caught! The toddler has boundless energy and ideas for play, developing self-reliance and confidence in exciting new abilities. The delightful cooing infant of a year ago has become a bossy, self-oriented toddler in constant motion!

Puzzles, toys such as nesting cans or cups, strings of snap beads, shaped toys which fit over spindles or into containers encourage the child to practice coordinating muscles and eyes. A varied selection of toys gives each child the opportunity to play at more than one ability level, thus being able to move on to new challenges whenever ready. Limit the number of toys which are available at any one time to avoid overwhelming the child with choices.

Emotional Development

Basic to a child's welfare is still a strong need to feel loved and accepted by adults. The toddler must feel love and acceptance even when doing things which are unacceptable. Show that you still love the child, even when you must redirect the child's behavior. When the toddler is behaving well, give specific praise as you identify specific acceptable actions: "Just look how still Joshua stands while I wash his face!"

As the child grows, the relationship between child and teacher becomes of greater importance than any activities. The toddler who has learned to love and trust adults is able to confidently explore and experience new elements in life. A toddler can build these quality relationships only with familiar adults who regularly provide loving care.

The toddler is aware of the emotional states of others and is sensitive to their expressions of anxiety. The child has a great desire to be loved and wants to show affection in return. By imitating the actions and attitudes of significant adults, the child establishes behavior patterns that will greatly influence the ongoing development of personality. For this reason toddlers need teachers who model Christ's love. Criteria for the selection of teachers should be as high for the Toddler Department as for any other group in the Sunday School.

In this seesaw world, the toddler inexpertly pushes to grow faster but then falls back on the love and support of familiar people. This drive for independence builds on the feelings of safety and love established as an infant. This active trust and sense of security provides a foundation to talk to the child about Jesus as someone who also loves and cares for him or her.

The toddler often tries to run the affairs of life without adult help, reaching for door knobs and marching up steps. The discovery of abilities is at the same time exciting and frightening. Bold, independent action is followed by a rush to the familiar security of the teacher or mother.

The strong desire for mother shows that her job of loving and caring has been well done. If the child cries when parents leave, assure the parents that this is because the child loves them, and is a positive sign.

A toddler tests limits in the process of learning new skills and building confidence. This often results in refusal to obey commands of adults the child loves. In a very real sense the toddler is battling for independence and selfhood. Teachers at church and parents at home must decide which things the child can do alone and which have to be restricted for the child's safety. The freedom to explore, test and try things out gives the child the feeling that life is something he or she can handle. Teachers need to respond to the child by listening attentively, expressing interest in what interests the child; by being fair in guiding and correcting the child. When it is necessary to stop a child's play, gently lead the child to a new activity. Avoid just saying, "No!"

At this age repetition and routine are critical. Retain the same room arrangement. Build on one major learning concept for a month at a time, selecting activities and songs that support that single thrust. Repeat the same basic learning experiences. Also, follow from Sunday to Sunday the same sequence through the morning. When the child feels able to predict what will happen next, a satisfying sense of control and security results.

The child approaching two continues to push out. At times the child may run away from a worker, scream in defiance, or simply decide not to cooperate in a most charming and disarming way. No matter how exasperating this may be, the toddler needs love, patience, kindness and firm, gentle control. In addition, the toddler needs time—time to go through this stage, for it cannot be bypassed. Avoid confrontations where possible, or situations which can develop into a battle of wills between you. Rather, give guidance indirectly by the arrangement of your materials and the flow of your activities.

For instance, if a child decides not to help or not come along when you call, continue the activity. The child's curiosity, the desire to be near adults, and the drive to be active will pull towards whatever you are doing regardless of any spoken no. Try whispering a suggestion to a child. The child may whisper back, enchanted with the air of mystery, eager to begin your new idea.

For many children toilet training is a very emotional issue. It is important to deal with "accidents" in a matter-of-fact way. Find out from parents if a child has a particular word to say when needing to use the toilet. Also be alert to physical signs such as fidgetiness. Remember that a young child cannot wait even a few seconds, so be prepared to have a teacher take a child out in the middle of an activity, if necessary. While some girls will be toilet trained before they turn two, most boys will not.

A toddler nearing the second birthday can begin to recognize some rights of others and make a few choices with other people in mind. The child who feels at ease and happy will be more cooperative. The child needs self-dignity and self-respect in order to have appreciation and esteem for others. With loving guidance and supervision, toddlers can play alongside each other although the desire to share and interact with others does not come until later. The young child can begin to help put toys away on storage shelves, but cannot do the job alone. As you work with a child in a task, take time for a friendly talk giving the child individual attention.

Learning

Young children do not wait for formal teaching situations before they learn. One of the nursery teacher's greatest opportunities to help a child is to capitalize on this learning potential. Little ones need to see, touch, smell, hear and taste to learn about their world and the people in it. Nature materials which the child can touch give support to your statements that, "God made this smooth rock . . . pretty flower, etc." Let children hear a seashell, feel lamb's wool, taste a banana, smell a pinecone and see brightly-colored pictures.

Brief conversation about the people and things in a child's world helps build an interest in God. Pictures of familiar objects help the child learn more about a variety of experiences. Show pictures of toys, church, plants, animals, and even people, and talk with the child about the pictures. Use short, simple sentences. Say, "Here is a bird. God made the bird," as you point to the pictured bird. Frequent conversations which include the child's name help the toddler grow in awareness of God and God's love. Repetition is essential to reinforce these concepts and ideas.

Imaginative play is a powerful learning experience which begins after the child is a year and a half old. The toddler expresses ideas and feelings, copies gestures and voice inflections, releases anger and frustration, relives experiences which are enjoyable or upsetting. A toddler is attracted to a doll and will hold, cuddle, rock and talk to it. A child can express with a doll familiar experiences of the child's own life. The doll can be a mother, father, brother or sister. When a child brings the doll to you, the gesture means, "Let's be friends. Come play with me."

Singing, chanting and impromptu storytelling using the child's name bring wholehearted response. The child responds to rhythm and made-up songs about the play activity. You can make up words to a tune the child knows to fit the activity you are doing together. For example, as Miss Tonsky sat looking at a book with three toddlers, she sang to the "Happy Birthday" tune, "I'm so glad Shannon's here, I'm so glad Tonya's here, I'm so glad Erin's here, and I'm glad I'm here, too." The fun you have together is far more important than the quality of your music or composition! The "Farmer in the Dell" and "Mulberry Bush" are also easy tunes to adapt.

Verbal Ability

Language becomes more important to the toddler with each passing month. For awhile the child uses a single word to express a complete thought. "Water," means, "I'm thirsty. I want a drink." As the child begins to talk, improvement occurs in the ability to retain what is spoken to the child. Opportunities for beginning prayer are natural now. There are "pretty flowers," "milk and cookies," "mommy and daddy," "our church" or "my friends" for which to thank God. Brief Bible thoughts such as "God cares about you," and "God made everything," may be used very simply in conversation and repeated over and over on a weekly basis. Praying aloud, even before the child can talk and join you, conveys that praying is important to you; and the child will want to pray just like you!

NOTE

1. Songs listed in this book are from *Fun-to-Sing, Little Ones Sing* or *Activity Songs for Young Children*. See Bibliography.

The Two- and Three-Year-Old

We were sitting in a circle on the floor. I was surrounded by six eager three-year-olds. I had my Bible open in front of me, and my flannelgraph figures arranged neatly beside me, ready to jump into action at the appropriate time.

I began the story of a man whose son was very sick. Oh, the pathos of the moment as I vividly described the child's illness and the father's anguish. Carefully I placed the father and son on the floor in the center of our little group.

Then I told of the father's long walk to find Jesus. I took the figure of the father and made him climb over shoes and down toes, up knees and down ankles. The suspense was building. We all felt the poor father's weariness as he pressed on to find the only person who could help his child.

Trevor couldn't take it any longer. Before I could intercept him, he lunged for my pile of additional flannelgraph figures and blurted out, "I wanna see Jesus."

Looking back on that incident, I was never quite sure if Trevor just wanted the story to be over or if he really had gotten so enthralled in my telling it that he wanted to help the poor father get to the end of his journey. Beyond either of those likely explanations, however, I am convinced Trevor was putting into words a common desire of two- and three-year-old children when they come into our classes. They want to see Jesus.

Jesus is a very appealing person to twos and threes. They love the story of Jesus inviting children to come to Him. They are drawn to His obvious compassion for those in need. They enjoy His stories about sheep and flowers and the kind man who helped an injured traveler. They love the songs that tell of Jesus' love for them.

TWO-YEAR-OLDS

Physical Development

The two-year-olds's body demands exercise. The child is constantly on the move—running, jumping and climbing. Because the large leg and arm muscles are rapidly developing, the child is often not sure of balance. Plan for open spaces in your room in which the child is free to move. Keep furnishings at a minimum. Provide equipment such as a rocking boat and climbing steps that allow the child to use large muscles. Use simple finger fun and activity songs that allow the child to reach and stretch, to jump and clap.

The two-year-old's small hand and finger muscles are not developed enough to allow sophisticated manipulation. For art activities, provide large sheets of blank paper and jumbo crayons or long-handled paintbrushes. (Do NOT expect the child to color within an outline!) Provide puzzles with a few large pieces; have large spools or beads to string. Provide large blocks or cartons the child can stack and manipulate.

The two-year-old tires easily. Constant activity is a source of real fatigue which is often the cause of unacceptable behavior. The child does not know how to stop and rest, so provide alternating times of active and quiet play. Be alert to the child who needs to "slow down." Gently redirect this child's attention to looking at a book or working a puzzle with you.

For example, Mrs. Lee watched as Jessica prepared to feed her doll at the Home Living area. She knew Jessica had been very active all morning and she noticed that Jessica was beginning to push away children who came too near.

Mrs. Lee said, "Jessica, your baby has had a good lunch. I think she'd like to hear a story. I have a new book she will like." Gently she took Jessica and her doll in her lap and together they looked at a picture book. As they sat quietly talking about the pictures, Jessica began to relax and was soon able to rejoin the other children.

Mental and Emotional Development

The two-year-old is an explorer rather than a creator. Trevor was watching the fish at the God's Wonders table. Suddenly, water was splashing everywhere as Trevor's hand went into the water and after the fish. Mr. Clark gently removed Trevor's hand from the bowl. As he dried Trevor and the tabletop, he said, "Our goldfish are for us to look at, not for us to touch. Watch the fish's tail move as he swims." As they watched together, Mr. Clark sang, "Who made the goldfish? God did . . . . " Mr. Clark knew Trevor was not being "bad." He was simply attempting to satisfy his curiosity about the fish.

The two-year-old's interest span is short. Expect a two to pick up a toy, drop it and move on to something else. Provide a variety of activities and do not expect a child to remain interested in any one thing for more than a few minutes.

The two-year-old's plea is, "let me do it!" Offer assistance only as needed. However, during an activity be alert for any child who might be reaching the point of frustration: step in with a suggestion to help the child succeed. "Ian, your puzzle has a pretty flower in it. I wonder if this piece will fit here." Then praise the child's successful attempts. Provide materials and equipment the child can easily manage.

The two-year-old sometimes says no when he or she means yes. The word a two-year-old hears most frequently is no! As a result, the child often uses the word because of its simplicity and familiarity. Phrase your suggestions in the form of statements, rather than questions. Avoid, "Do you want to . . . ?" Rather say, "Please bring the book to me. Thank you, Juan."

The two-year-old's vocabulary is increasing, sometimes using words without understanding. The child doesn't always mean what the words say! When talking with the two-year-old use simple words and short sentences. Avoid symbolism! Speak slowly and clearly, without "talking down" to the child. The child enjoys listening to songs, finger fun and rhythms, asking to hear favorites over and over again.

The two-year-old is still very self-centered. Everything the child does relates to self. Sing songs that include the child's name, such as, "Who made Devon? God did .... " Use the child's name often in your conversation. When a child talks to you, look into the child's face and give your undivided attention.

The two-year-old has little sense of time, and can't be hurried. Do not expect an immediate response to your requests. Allow plenty of time for moving from one part of the schedule to the next; for putting on coats, for wash-up and toilet details.

Social Development

The two-year-old has little regard for the rights of others. At times it seems as if *no* and *mine* are the only words the two knows! Sharing and taking turns are new words and new ideas to most twos. When disputes occur, a two will more likely respond to distraction than to reasoning. "Chris, that's Eric's truck. Here is a red truck for you to use." Provide duplicates of favorite toys.

The two-year-old seeks close physical contact with loving, understanding adults. Jesus called little children to Him and rebuked those who would send them away. We can easily imagine that He held them on His lap and listened patiently to their chatter. Those who guide twos need to be kind, patient Christians who love little children and who are willing to give the kind of attention the child's behavior shows is needed. A smile and a friendly pat might meet the needs of one child while a hug or a few moments of cuddling might be the answer for another. An effective teacher knows the needs of the children and is able to respond to those needs.

The two-year-old's moments of fear, disappointment and frustration require the help of an understanding adult. Should a child cry when mother leaves, avoid shaming or disapproving remarks. Help the child feel secure by giving warm, personal attention, such as holding the child on your lap as you look at a book. Ask mother to leave something, such as a sweater or a scarf to help assure the child she will return.

The two-year-old comes to you on Sunday morning with the potential to learn many things. If you prepare your room and thoughts ahead of time, the child will learn and grow in wisdom and stature and in favor with God and man. (See Luke 2:52.)

Milestones of Development

The ability to talk is the dominant advance made by the child between 18 months and three years. The child is changing rapidly during this period and is characterized by a bountiful and boundless energy that adults often wish they could harness. The child is a demanding runabout who requires all of the stamina, creativity and patience the learning leader has to give.

By two years of age the child may:
- be walking and climbing on chairs and stairs, always on the go!
- scribble on paper spontaneously and vigorously (the wall, too, if you're not careful), and imitate your strokes with crayon;
- use words in one- and two-word sentences;
- point to nose, eyes, hair, ears when asked to identify them;
- build a high tower with blocks;
- fill a container with smaller objects;
- handle and chew crackers and other finger food at snack times;
- turn pages of book to look at pictures;
- throw a ball into a box.

Between the ages of two and three years the child may:
- run and play with great energy;
- tire easily, becoming fussy and irritable;
- say many words and make sentences of several words;
- understand most normal conversation;
- be interested in everything everywhere all the time;
- play happily alone, with occasional interaction with others;

- be bowel-trained and have daytime bladder control;
- know where objects belong and help to put them away;
- follow one direction at a time.

THREE-YEAR-OLDS

Physical Development

The three-year-old is developing effective large muscle control, and is sure on his feet, with an accurate sense of his limits. The child enjoys active experiences and materials, such as blocks for building, that encourage the use of large muscles. The child needs room in which to move about, so keep furnishings to a minimum. Provide a choice of activities and freedom to move from one activity to another.

The three-year-old's control of small finger and hand muscles is not developed to allow cutting accurately with scissors or coloring within an outline. The child is ready to experiment with glue; collages are a great activity. The three enjoys beads to string and puzzles to solve. Provide pegs and pegboards and a wide variety of utensils to use with clay. Repeat familiar activities often as they support Bible aims.

Three-year-olds play hard and tire easily. Provide a balance of active and quiet play. Be alert to the child who is becoming over-stimulated. Guide this child to a quiet activity, such as working a puzzle or looking at a picture book with you. During the second hour of the morning, plan for a rest time of not less than 10 minutes. Include a light snack, also.

Mental and Emotional Development

Imaginative play begins to flower during this year. Simple imitation of an adult example gradually develops into extended efforts to be "Mommy," "Daddy," "Fire fighter" or "Teacher." There is little true interaction in this play, and several "mommies" are likely to occupy the Home Living center at one time. However, the child's ability to imagine being someone else is an important step forward in mental growth.

The three-year-old participates only as long as interest remains. A variety of activities is necessary to meet constantly changing levels of attention. As Mrs. Graham told a story of ways God planned for food to grow, she noticed that some children were becoming restless. Without stopping her story, she said, "And God planned for apples to grow on trees. Let's pretend we are apple trees and stretch our branches way up into the sky . . . . Let's pretend the wind is blowing our branches . . . . " As the children moved their arms high overhead, she sang, "The apple trees are swaying . . . . " When the song ended and everyone sat down again, she showed a food picture and continued her story by saying, "Look what else God made that's good to eat!"

Mrs. Graham recognized two needs: (1) the children's need to stretch and move, and (2) her need to regain the children's attention. Both needs were met by giving the children an opportunity to sing and move. They were actively participating in the story. The second need was met by immediately drawing the children's attention to the picture.

Children also listen better when they have first had an opportunity to share their ideas. Then require them to listen quietly as you take your turn. Keep your turn brief, however. A good rule of thumb for story length with young children is one minute for each year of age.

A three-year-old does not understand symbolism! Use simple stories told in literal terms—words that mean exactly what they say.

The child also may have difficulty understanding directions. Give one brief direction at a time. Allow a child to complete the task before suggesting the next one. Rather than saying, "Pick up the toys, then go sit down," say, "It's time to put the toys on this shelf." Work with the children, commending them for their efforts. As they finish, say, "Thank you for putting every toy in just the right place. Now it's time to sit on the rug and sing some songs." The leader should begin some activity songs while children are gathering. The music will draw the more reticent and occupy those who have cooperated immediately.

Social Development

The three-year-old is sensitive to your actions, attitudes and feelings. It is important for you to know each child as an individual. Jesus was keenly aware of people as individuals. For instance, when He was surrounded by those who had come to see Him, He stopped and called Zacchaeus—by name! You represent that highly personal love of God to the young child.

As Sean and his family rode home from church, he announced, "God didn't come to Sunday School today." After a moment of silence, he added, "But He sent my teacher." To the young child you are God's representative. Help the child to know of God's love by loving the child yourself. Help the child to know Jesus as a kind, loving friend, by being a good listener.

Jeremy was trying earnestly to tell his teacher something he considered of great importance. His teacher kept on preparing materials for another part of the morning schedule, occasionally offering a noncommittal "uh-huh." Finally, in desperation Jeremy said, "Listen to me!"

"I *am* listening," his teacher replied.

"But you're not listening with your face!" was Jeremy's comment.

Jeremy in his three-year-old way distinguished between having someone merely hear his words and someone listen to him attentively. When you talk with a child, sit or bend down so you are at eye level, give your undivided attention (stop what you are doing), respond to the child's words by sharing the child's enthusiasm or offering a bit of sympathy. As you show genuine interest in each child, you are demonstrating God's love in a way the child can understand. The Lord Jesus' command that we love one another becomes alive with meaning. God's Word demonstrated is more convincing to young children than God's Word explained.

The three-year-old still likes to play alone but also enjoys being with other children. While the three-year-old has not left self-centered "me, my and mine" world, frequent parallel play often advances into real interaction and cooperation. Offer activities that allow the child to participate successfully alongside other children, with opportunities available for interaction.

Three-year-olds often lack the language to begin a conversation. Instead they say, "Hi, play with me," by bumping the other child or grabbing at toys. Create opportunities that foster healthy social development. For instance, "Lana, you really have lots of pegs. I think Brandon needs some more pegs. What can you do to help Brandon? . . . You are a kind friend to share pegs with Brandon."

Provide activities that encourage children to relate to one another. Identify and interpret specific acts of kindness so a child knows what to do to be loving and friendly. Be ready with words of praise and encouragement when a child exhibits acceptable behavior toward another child.

Sharing and taking turns are still hard for most three-year-olds. Identify what these words mean. "First I roll the ball to Marta. Marta rolls it back to me. Now I roll it to Suni. We're taking turns!" Be sure that each child gets a turn so that taking turns doesn't come to mean losing out!

Before a child can relate satisfactorily to others, he or she needs to feel good about self. Help develop self-confidence and a healthy self-image by providing experiences in which each child can succeed, being careful to introduce activities that will challenge rapidly developing abilities. Kevin had successfully put together every puzzle in the rack several times in recent weeks. Miss Payne commented on his achievement as she brought out two new puzzles, each with several more pieces than the others. The new challenge restimulated Kevin's interest in doing puzzles. More important, Kevin learned another lesson that built his confidence—and his thankfulness to God for "giving Kevin hands and eyes to do puzzles."

Milestones of Development

To a child between three and four years old, everything is a beautiful, fascinating mystery just waiting to be solved. The child is full of whys, mischievousness, imagination and willingness, all waiting to be challenged.

Between three and four years old the child may:
- unbutton and button large side and front buttons;
- unlace and take off shoes;
- put on shoes if someone holds the tongues down;
- put on and take off galoshes, if they're large enough to slip easily over shoes;
- build actual structures with blocks;
- begin to draw and paint simple pictures of objects and people;
- begin to use numbers to count objects;
- learn nursery rhymes, songs and finger fun;
- use scissors to cut on heavy, straight lines;
- interact with others in imaginative play;
- recognize his or her name in print, and write at least part of it;
- identify primary colors by name;
- take care of most toilet needs.

Notes:

The Four- and Five-Year-Old

The eight little boys all had two things in common. They were all five years old and they had on the same colored shirt. That seemed to be where all similarities stopped.

They did seem aware that they were all supposed to be on the same soccer team, working together toward the common goal of kicking the ball into the net marked with the same color as their shirts. There were several who were very intent on that objective. Several others showed occasional interest in kicking the ball if it came near them, but they did not seem concerned about which direction they happened to kick it. One boy was fascinated with an airplane barely visible on the far horizon. Another was busy waving at Grandpa operating his video camera. Two were having a great deal of fun shoving each other around a mud puddle that had accumulated around a sprinkler head in the grass.

As long as the coaches and parents and referees were content to allow the boys to have fun at their own speed, they all thoroughly enjoyed "playing soccer." But when the grown-ups tried to corral the boys into paying attention and working as a team (along with other adult objectives), then tempers became short on both sides of the generation gap. Proudly watching my son as one of the minority on either team who seemed to care about scoring goals, I muttered, "You can put the boys on the team, but you can't put the team in the boys."

That remark seemed profound at the time, but it does illustrate one of the intriguing features of four- and five-year-olds. They can look—and even act—so mature at one moment that we start to think of them as "big kids, really growing up." And the next moment they remind us that they are just a few months removed from the baby and toddler and three-year-old who desperately need the comforting presence of a caring adult.

FOUR-YEAR-OLDS

The four-year-old is much advanced in abilities but very similar in needs to a three-year-old. Both age groups need to explore new materials but their use of them varies greatly depending on the individual level of skill development.

Physical Development

The four-year-old is in the child period of rapid physical growth. Coordination improves and is stronger and more confident than at three. The four-year-old still seems to be constantly on the go—running, jumping, walking or climbing, needing open spaces to move about freely.

Freehand, creative art activities are the most satisfying. Continue to provide large sheets of paper and large crayons. (Do not expect a four-year-old to color within lines!) Some four-year-olds may begin to draw pictures such as a face, a flower, a house. At the paint easel the child uses a large brush to make sweeping strokes of bright color.

Because the four-year-old is gaining control of the small muscles, there is real enjoyment in attempting activities that involve fine coordination. Provide opportunities to button, zip a zipper, lace shoes and cut on a heavy line. Make them fun by letting the child practice and not drawing attention to performance, but rather to perseverance.

Like the three-year-old, the four-year-old tires quickly. Rapid growth and constant activity cause easy fatigue. This tiredness may result in unacceptable behavior. Alternate times of active and quiet play throughout your morning schedule.

Mental and Emotional Development

The four-year-old has a strong desire to learn reasons for everything. The child is curious and questioning. The favorite words for fours seem to be *how, what* and *why.* Fours also enjoy experimenting with words. Making up silly-sounding rhymes is great fun and gives good practice in improving language skills. While questions are common, most learning continues in much the same way as before—by doing. Continue to provide materials for children to touch, smell, see and even taste. Use everyday objects and activities to relate Scripture truths to the child's life. Use simple words and literal phrases that mean exactly what they say.

The four-year-old can concentrate for longer periods of time than at three. However, the attention span is still short. The child is easily distracted and the rapidly developing large muscles make it difficult to sit quietly for more than four or five minutes. Provide a variety of activities and materials, selecting those most appropriate to specific learning aims. For example, one Sunday you may provide puzzles. The next Sunday you could lead a matching game. Make changes from one hour to the next, also. During Sunday School the Home Living center may be involved in doll play, then during Churchtime, a food preparation activity could be used. Rotation of activities saves money, wear and tear on supplies, and adds variety. Never change everything at once. One or two different activities is adequate. This retains the flavor of the room while simultaneously adding interest.

The four-year-old has advanced considerably in one year in the ability to participate with other children in group activities. Because of a limited attention span, group activities should still be kept brief. Provide group singing, prayer and conversation about activities just finished. Use large teaching pictures to reinforce basic concepts.

The four-year-old is often testing the world. The child may exhibit unacceptable behavior just to see how far he or she can go. The child finds security in the very limits being defied; yet limits should not hinder the freedom to experiment. Be consistent in your every-Sunday guidance. Be positive in your suggestions. Emphasize the behavior you desire rather than the kind you want to discourage. Say, "We keep the blocks in the block area" rather than "Don't bring the blocks to the home corner!" The word "don't" often makes a child want to resist.

A four can often write at least part of his or her first name. The four will want to do as much of it as possible, and will watch intensely whenever you write it for him or her. Print the child's name clearly, using a capital followed by lower case letters. If a child is interested, form a dot pattern which the child can trace.

The four-year-old may exaggerate his or her abilities: "I can climb to the very top of this building; I can run and jump better than anyone else!" Do not dispute these claims, but redirect the conversation. "You can run and jump because your legs are growing strong, just as God planned. I need a strong boy like you to help put these blocks away."

Social Development

The four-year-old longs for and actively seeks adult approval. The child responds to friendliness and wants to be loved, especially by you, the teacher. Be interested in what interests the child and in what the child has to say. Be ready with a friendly, personal greeting: "That's a bright orange shirt you're wearing, Kevin. Is it new? . . . I like the stripes."

Give the child opportunities to lead, with your support. For example, let a child serve a snack or hold a picture. This will build confidence.

The four-year-old shows a growing interest in doing things with other children. While younger fours may still prefer to work alone or in parallel play, older fours enjoy working in small groups of two or three children.

The four-year-old likes to pretend. "I'm the daddy and you're the mother" kinds of play occur frequently in the Home Living area as children now begin to interact in simple family roles. Children also like to play out experiences. "We're going to the park today. Everybody get ready," a four is likely to announce.

Provide both male and female clothing and accessories for dress up.

FIVE- AND SIX-YEAR-OLDS

While a large number of three- and four-year-olds attend day-care centers and nursery schools, in many regions most, if not all, fives attend kindergarten. The child who experiences regular group experiences will tend to have advantages in terms of inter-action with other children, ability to participate in a group and skill in using common learning materials. However, the basic developmental *sequence* will remain the same for all children. Since most children will turn six before they move on to first grade, it is important to be aware of the continuing development of the six-year-old child.

Physical Development

The five- and six-year-old is still physically active. Strength, agility and balance are well coordinated, and develop at an equal rate. The child still needs opportunities for movement of body, arms and legs. Dramatic play, finger fun and activity songs encourage jumping, stretching and bending. Block building is an excellent every-Sunday learning activity. Fives and sixes need plenty of room in which to move about, so keep furnishings in the room to a minimum.

Freehand drawing and painting with large crayons or brushes is still most appropriate. Also provide clay or salt/flour dough for the children to use. Alternate active and quiet experiences so children are not required to sit still for more than four or five minutes.

While the child's growth rate is slowing, girls are maturing more rapidly than boys in their physical development. Expect boys to become restless sooner during a large group activity.

Small muscles are now under better control than at four. The child enjoys more sophisticated toys and is getting close to being able to color accurately within lines. Also, cutting accurately is still difficult for fives, although they can follow a simple, curved line. Six-year-olds can cut more complicated shapes.

Mental and Emotional Development

The five- and six-year-old likes to help and thrives on the approval and attention received from adults and peers. Helping tasks such as bringing materials from the art shelf or carrying scraps to the wastebasket also help the child work off some excess energy. Give responsibilities which the child can perform successfully. Offer praise when a child completes a task.

As children were finishing making cookies at the Home Living table, Mr. Walters said, "Nathan, the table is sticky. What do you think we should do?"

"Wash it off," Nathan replied.

"Good thinking, Nathan. Can you find a wet sponge to use?" Nathan looked around and spotted a sponge next to the dishpan of water Mr. Walters had brought to the room. He quickly dipped the sponge in the water and thoroughly scrubbed the table.

"Nathan, you know where to find the sponge and you know how to clean the table. You have learned to use your mind and your arms to help just like the Bible says. Can you remember what the Bible says about helping?"

"'With love, help one another,'" Nathan responded. He had heard Mr. Walters use that verse several times as they were making cookies. Not only could he repeat it, he could demonstrate it!

Five- and six-year-olds will stay with some activities longer than younger children. One Sunday Laticia spent the total Bible Learning Activity Time in the Home Living corner, caring for dolls and setting the table. The next week, however, she started at the painting easel, moved to the book shelf, looked through the magnifying glass in God's Wonders, then returned to the book shelf. Choices of activities provide for these variations in each child's interests.

Most five- and six-year-olds are learning to write (print) in kindergarten. Be aware of each child's level of accomplishment. Be careful to praise each child for what he or she can do and not compare children with each other.

Kindergarten is an introduction into the academic world of numbers, letters and a few simple words. Activities that contribute directly to beginning reading skills include blocks, puzzles and matching games, all of which help a child's awareness of shape and size relationships. Books are also important in building interest in reading. Art activities can be enriched by letting the child dictate comments about the picture which the teacher can attach to the paper. Also, make word cards and tape them to objects around the room. Use words like Bible, Picture, Blocks, Window, Coats, etc. Refer to them from time to time and the children will begin to "read" them.

The child is curious, eager to learn and asks many questions. Answer questions in ways that will stimulate the child's own thinking. Michael was using the magnet at the God's Wonders table. "Why won't the magnet pick up this box?" he asked.

"Let's see if we can find out," answered Mrs. Van Dyk. "Will it pick up this nail?" Together, Mrs. Van Dyk and Michael tried to pick up various objects with the magnet. As they worked, Mrs. Van Dyk stimulated Michael's thinking until he reached the conclusion that a magnet only picks up certain kinds of metal.

The child still relies on the five senses for learning. Use objects the child can see, touch, smell, taste and hear.

The five- and six-year-old still interprets words literally, not understanding symbolic concepts. Use words that mean exactly what they say. Instead of singing a symbolic song, such as, "The B-I-B-L-E," sing "Our Bible:"

"Our Bible tells how God loves us,
God loves us,
God loves us.
Our Bible tells how God loves us,
how God loves you and me."

The child still needs affection and security. While sometimes appearing to be strong and confident, the child is still easily upset and needs dependable adult support. A child can go quickly from bravado to tears or from tears to laughter. This does not mean the feelings are shallow. It means the child is still a child of the immediate present.

Social Development

The child needs attention from other children and adults. Stacy thought she had found a way to win approval by tattling. Her teacher wisely just said, "I know you want children to do right things. You do what is right so the others can watch you and copy you."

Give the child individual attention before any negative behavior occurs. Initiate conversations, listen closely when a child talks to you. Give a smile, a hug or a pat on the shoulder to show your affection and interest. This will reduce the need for negative attention-getting.

The five- and six-year-old enjoys working in small groups with much real cooperation occurring. However, when more than two or three children participate in an activity, adult help is needed to insure that every child can be involved. Even when only two or three play together, adult help is often needed to suggest ideas that will keep the activity moving.

One Sunday, Mr. Gomez planned an activity to encourage thankfulness for food. He posted on the bulletin board a long sheet of butcher paper divided into three sections: Breakfast, Lunch, Dinner. He provided food pictures torn from magazines, scissors to trim the pictures, and glue. The children selected pictures of food for which they were thankful. There was considerable conversation among the children as they decided whether certain pictures went better under "breakfast" or "lunch." As they worked, Mr. Gomez commented that God made our food. He expressed his own thanks to God for it and gave opportunity for the children to do so also.

The children in your department come from different and varied backgrounds. There will be children from Christian homes where the love of God is a natural part of everyday conversation. There will be children who have never heard about God's love. There will be children who have been in Sunday School since birth and there will be those who are attending for the first time. Begin where the child is; plan experiences which can relate the richness of God's love. "Teach a child to choose the right path, and when he is older he will remain upon it" (Prov. 22:6, *TLB*).

Milestones of Development

Between the ages of four and six, the child may:

- tie shoelaces, though not always tight enough to stay;
- participate in extended cooperative play with one or two friends;
- write his or her name clearly without help;
- read some simple words;
- cut with scissors along a curved line;
- draw or paint easily recognizable pictures of people and objects;
- recognize tints and shades of common colors;
- recall short Bible verses which have been heard frequently;
- talk accurately about recent events;
- pronounce most common words correctly.

PART 2

Organizing for Successful Teaching

Becoming an Effective Teacher

In the bustle of a busy convention exhibit hall, I bumped into a woman I had not seen for over ten years. She asked me if I remembered Doug and pulled out her wallet to show me a picture of her tall, good-looking teenage son. I tried to connect the face of this young man with my memory of Doug, a child I had taught in the four- and five-year-old Sunday School class. His mother began to tell me about Doug's steady growth as a Christian, his involvement in his church youth group, his participation in Bible study. And then she shocked me: "It all began that year he was in your Sunday School class."

"R-r-really?" I stammered. "How do you mean?"

"Well," she explained, "until that year, he had always disliked Sunday School and church. Your class was the first one he enjoyed, the first time he ever wanted to attend. Whatever you did that year got him interested. And he's loved being at church ever since."

I have pondered that conversation many times trying to recall the "whatever" that had clicked with Doug. When was the moment that Doug began to respond? What was the lesson or the activity or the conversation that first reached him? But nowhere in my recollection of Doug is there any awareness of something significant happening to make a change in him.

There is a part of me that does wish I could recall an electric moment, a morning when I noticed Doug and said just the right words in the right way and overcame his dislike of Sunday School. I do wish I could remember speaking to Doug and seeing something in his eyes that said, "Thanks, Wes, you've just made a big difference in my life."

However, another part of me recognizes that it is probably better that I not know what "clicked" with Doug. First, because I would probably tend to use the same approach on every other child I've taught in the years since. And second, because it reminds me that God works through a teacher in ways the teacher often does not know. If God has only worked through my teaching in those moments when I felt something special was happening, I would be extremely discouraged about all those times when all I felt was tired.

Becoming an effective teacher, a teacher through whom God touches a child's life, is only partly a matter of the methods and mechanics of leading a group. Becoming an effective teacher is primarily a matter of becoming a person who nurtures a growing relationship with God. When God is working *in* you, He will then be able to work *through* you.

While modern society has found many instant approaches to formerly time-consuming tasks (instant potatoes, instant tea, instant oatmeal, etc.), there is no shortcut to building a relationship with God. While there are many variations in pursuing personal and spiritual growth, there are also some constants which need to be nourished:

1. *Personal time with God in prayer and Bible reading.* Most people find they need to make this time a priority in setting their schedules, otherwise it simply gets squeezed out by all the other details of daily life.

2. *Supportive time with God's people.* Every believer needs other believers, especially a small group which will provide caring and accountability to one another.

3. *Productive time for ministry.* Teaching is one of God's highest callings and deserves to be given our best, not our remainders.

A person who is working to build these life patterns is laying a solid foundation on which to build effective teaching skills.

TEACHER

Early Childhood teachers are:
- Creators of an environment where children can learn;
- Sources of love;
- Models for children to emulate;
- Guides in learning experiences;
- Partners with parents in nurturing a child's growth;
- Very Special People!

Teachers of two-year-olds through five-year-olds:
- Prepare and guide one Bible learning activity for each session.
- Prepare (and if possible present the Bible story each week to a small class group) and guide children in completing their activity pages.
- Participate in large group activities and transitions between activities.

Teachers of babies and toddlers:
- Prepare interaction activities appropriate to children's development and unit learning aims, creating a safe, interesting environment.
- Focus primary attention for care and interaction on a small group of children as assigned by leader.
- Assist with other children as necessary.

All Sunday School teachers:
- Pray regularly for class members and families.
- Maintain home contact with class members and families.
- Attend and participate in regular departmental planning meetings.
- Take advantage of training opportunities to improve teaching skills.

The Teacher's Morning ■ Teachers arrive on Sunday morning in time to set up activity areas before the first child arrives. This usually means arriving at least 15 minutes before the session is scheduled to begin. As children arrive, they immediately choose a Bible learning activity. The teacher at each activity guides the children in learning experiences related to the lesson's Bible aim. Baby and toddler teachers move among the activities, caring primarily for the children assigned to them. Each teacher's specific responsibility is determined at the department planning meeting.

Following these Bible learning activities, teachers of twos through fives guide children in putting away materials, then moving together for group singing and sharing. The teachers sit among the children as the Department Leader directs the group. Group experiences with toddlers often occur spontaneously, as when one teacher sings a song and the children come over to investigate.

Because children need to find security in a close relationship with one adult, each teacher of twos through fives is assigned a small class group. The teacher tells the Bible story to the same class group each Sunday unless the story is told in the large, department group. Continuing relationship with an individual teacher helps a child feel loved and special.

After the Bible story, the Bible teaching/learning objective is reinforced by an activity page used in the small class groups. The teacher shows a completed page, talks about the truth it illustrates, then guides children in completing their own pages. Thus each child has an opportunity to respond to the truth that was emphasized in the Bible story.

Teachers continue with the children until the Churchtime (or second-hour) staff is ready to assume leadership.

The Teacher's Week ■ *Preparation:* Teaching young children involves more than simply being in the room during the session. Thoughtful planning is necessary to make sure the activities provided produce positive learning. Each teacher needs to spend time each week in study of the Bible passage and the curriculum materials. Without this planning, the teacher's effectiveness will diminish and many learning opportunities will be lost.

No teacher works alone. Each is a part of the whole ministry of the church and Sunday School. Meeting together at the start of each unit of lessons to plan, pray and share is vitally necessary to all teachers.

Parents: Children are in an Early Childhood department for only an hour or two each week. They spend the major share of their time at home. True concern for the child's spiritual life, therefore, compels a teacher to cultivate a relationship with the parents, sharing with them the objectives of the department and concern for their child's spiritual growth. Evidence that someone cares about their child will draw many parents closer to the church and to God. Noticing absences and remembering birthdays shows parents and children the teacher really cares. A bridge of mutual trust and understanding between church and home is built in this manner, opening doors for teachers to share the reality of Christian faith.

Be aware of homes in the neighborhood in which there are small children who do not attend Sunday School. Personal contacts that show a loving concern for these children may result in parents bringing these children to Sunday School. Such contacts have often resulted in entire families being won to Christ.

DEPARTMENT LEADER

A department with three or more teachers needs a *Department Leader* (or Lead Teacher). A smaller department may operate with two teachers informally sharing the leadership responsibilities. Each Department Leader works within a department guiding both teachers and children. The leader should have experiences as a teacher in order to provide both instruction and example in fulfilling these duties:

1. Coordinate and evaluate all activities within the department.

2. Lead the large group activities of the department.

3. Insure that each child receives a personal greeting at the door.

4. Suggest prospective new staff for the department.

5. Maintain proper teacher-pupil ratios.

6. Lead teachers in building relationships with families, seeking to win those who are unsaved.

7. Recommend space, equipment and material needs of the department.

8. Communicate necessary information among the staff.

9. Organize and lead regular department planning meetings.

10. Communicate regularly with Churchtime staff to coordinate the Churchtime and Sunday School plans.

Supporting the Team ■ The Department Leader should be alert to the way the entire Sunday morning program is being conducted. Compliments for jobs well done give teachers a sense of satisfaction in their work. Constructive suggestions, tactfully given, will always be appreciated by concerned teachers. Leaders need to encourage teachers to try new, well-planned techniques that will help them achieve a greater measure of success. Leaders also need to listen attentively to teachers' suggestions and complaints; then make an attempt to incorporate any constructive ideas.

Guiding Bible Learning Activities ■ The Department Leader should greet children when they first arrive. The first moments a child is in the room set the tone for the rest of the child's morning. Greet each child by name, bending or squatting to eye level. Assist as necessary in hanging up a coat or sweater and putting on a name tag.

Invite the child to the Love Gift center, then explain the Bible learning activities. "Which would you like to do first?" is a good question to ask. If the child is shy or crying, looking at a book while sitting on a teacher's lap is often effective in providing needed security.

As teachers and children work on Bible learning activities, the leader should be ready to deal with any problems that arise. Typical situations needing the leader's help include: a child reluctant to participate; a crying child; too many children in one area; a behavior problem. As the leader meets these needs there are many opportunities to talk informally with both children and teachers, setting a positive, friendly tone for the whole room. The leader is thus able to observe teacher's strengths and weaknesses without being threatening to the teacher.

Organizing Together Time ■ The Department Leader gives the signal when it is time to move to the large group. The leader begins an activity song or finger fun as the first children arrive at the circle. This frees the teachers to assist slower children in finishing cleanup before all join the large group. The leader's observation of the activity groups makes it easy to relate songs and other features to the activities children have just completed.

From week to week, one or other of the teachers may assist in some aspect of the large group time. A team effort will enrich this time for the children and help teachers improve their capabilities.

Supporting Bible Story Time ■ If teachers meet with their small groups to tell the Bible story, the leader is available to assist as needed, especially when a restless child needs a calming hand on the shoulder or a whisper in the ear. In some cases it is necessary to remove a child. The leader can look at books with him, insuring that the child is still allowed to learn.

If the story is told in the department group, the leader should use the story presentation to model good communication skills for the teachers. In this situation, consider rotating the story presentation among all the staff members.

The Department Leader also directs teachers in providing a smooth transition into Churchtime.

Filling Personnel Needs ■ The Department Leader is aware of the department's personnel requirements and should be involved in seeking additional staff when the need arises. The leader should work closely with the Division Coordinator or General Superintendent in order to maintain a proper teacher/pupil ratio within the department. Through the course of the year a department's attendance may change enough to warrant adding teachers or even starting a new department. Leaders should be alert to this situation so proper action can be taken in time to maintain a good quality program.

Evaluate Facilities ■ The leader can recommend and implement many improvements and help upgrade materials and equipment. The problem of inadequate facilities can rarely be corrected quickly or simply. A leader who knows what is needed and why it is needed can make solid and realistic recommendations for improvement which fit the church's budget. Often Early Childhood church leaders allow facility problems to exist simply because no one who works directly in the program takes the initiative to make positive suggestions.

Reaching Homes ■ Good communication between teachers and parents is essential in order to build home and church into an effective teaching partnership. The Department Leader must encourage parents and teachers to get together. Invite the parents to come and observe your program. This will help the children adjust and also build a bond with the families. To lead the department in effective outreach, the leader should set an example in contacting and visiting homes.

The leader should also seek to develop a good working relationship with the young adult classes attended by children's parents. As new families bring their children to an Early Childhood department, the leader needs to alert the appropriate adult class to these potential new members.

Many Department Leaders find the task of working with parents deserves enlisting someone to focus on this specific ministry. Often called an Outreach Leader, this person works alongside the Department Leader. (See Outreach Leader section below.)

Regular Planning Meetings ■ Much of the success of an Early Childhood department, regardless of size, depends on good relationships among its staff. The Department Leader needs to meet regularly with the entire department staff for prayer, evaluation and planning. Some departments meet every week to get ready for the next Sunday. Many others meet once at the beginning of every unit to coordinate the efforts of each person on the team. A unit planning meeting saves time by allowing the staff to survey four or five lessons at one time.

The Department Leader should also talk individually with teachers between meetings. This keeps the department operating smoothly and provides opportunity for the leader to share insights gained from observation during the Sunday sessions.

A UNIT PLANNING MEETING FOR AN EARLY CHILDHOOD DEPARTMENT

7:00 Ministry to Each Other
- Study of Bible passage to be taught to children
- Sharing of personal victories and challenges
- Prayer for each other's needs

7:30 Teacher Improvement Feature
- Focus on one skill each month (music, storytelling, discipline, creative art, blocks, etc.)
- Evaluate previous unit in light of this skill

8:00 Preview New Unit
- Bible Aims
- Bible coverage—Main thrust of stories
- Bible verses
- Music to support aims
- Bible learning activity assignments

8:30 Plan First Lesson of Unit
- Lesson Aims
- Bible learning activity materials and conversation
- Bible story ideas and resources
- Activity page

9:00 Dismiss

GENERAL SUPERINTENDENT AND DIVISION COORDINATOR

The **General Superintendent** is responsible to the church for the work of the Sunday School. In many churches this person is elected by the church to work closely with every Department Leader. Some churches assign this leadership role to a paid staff member (Director or Minister of Education).

A **Division Coordinator** should be appointed when a church has three or more Early Childhood departments. This leader is responsible to the General Superintendent and assumes direction for all functions in this division. The coordinator works closely with the department leader, guiding by suggestion and demonstration to make the teaching/learning in these departments more effective.

Both the General Superintendent and Division Coordinator must be knowledgeable in Early Childhood education in order to guide other people in their work. The main leadership tasks are:

1. Lead the division (made up of all the Early Childhood departments) in planning, conducting and evaluating its work.

2. Communicate to the division the goals of the church in areas such as: curriculum, outreach, teacher standards, relationships with parents, etc.

3. Lead teachers in setting goals for improvement and in evaluating progress toward these goals.

4. Work with department leaders in enlisting and training new staff in accordance with church policy.

5. Guide leaders of Sunday School and Churchtime in providing a coordinated total morning program.

6. Work with department leaders to insure in-service training for current staff through regular planning meetings.

7. Lead in evaluating and improving facilities and other needed resources.

8. Coordinate with other church agencies to develop a well-balanced program of Christian education.

A SAMPLE EARLY CHILDHOOD DIVISION

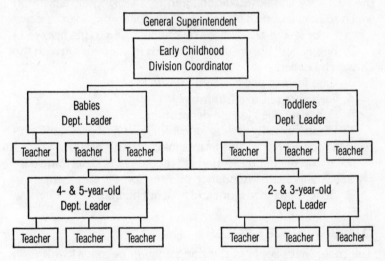

OUTREACH LEADER

Many effective teachers lack the time and confidence to make phone calls and home visits to prospects and visitors. And many Christians have a desire to be used in winning people to Christ and the church, but feel very inadequate to lead a group of children. The Outreach Leader in a department can relieve teachers of the responsibility for prospect and visitor follow-up. Once a child begins to attend regularly, the Outreach Leader can assign that child to a teacher for any further home contacts. The Outreach Leader then can encourage and remind teachers to follow up absentees and remember birthdays.

SECRETARY

Sunday School efficiency depends on accurate records. Secretaries need to keep track of children and supplies to make possible an orderly and effective ministry. The secretary can assist the teachers by doing some or all of these important tasks.

1. Arrive before the first child to greet and sign in each child. (If the Department Leader must guide a Bible learning activity, the secretary should guide children in choosing an activity in which to begin work. The secretary can often provide the comfort a shy or fearful child needs before choosing to get involved.)

2. Keep accurate, up-to-date records in cooperation with the Outreach Leader.

3. Care for and use children's name tags.

4. Take care of Love Gift money.

5. Order supplies for the department.

6. Prepare activity sheets for Bible Story groups. (Many secretaries secure help on this from senior citizen's groups.)

7. Attend planning meetings to record plans, determine supply needs and share attendance information with teachers.

8. Send cards to visitors and absent children.

OTHER MINISTRY ROLES

The more that people in the congregation become involved in some way with your Early Childhood ministries, the stronger your program will be. Consider these ideas of other ways people can serve in your department:

Prayer Partners ■ People who agree to pray regularly for a specific teacher and/or child. These people should be given periodic information about things being done in your group.

Huggers ■ Toddlers, twos and threes often find separation from parent a very difficult experience. A warm, friendly hug from a familiar person can make a big difference. A hugger stays near the door to help welcome arriving children and focuses on any having a hard time. Older adults make terrific huggers.

Rockers ■ Every Baby/Toddler department could use a gentle person to hold and rock a little one who is tired, fussy or in need of a bottle. Many people will volunteer for this level of comforting care as long as the other needs of the department are adequately covered by the remaining staff.

Room Mom or Dad ■ This person agrees to assist the Department Leader in several clearly defined ways. It's best to choose a parent who is well-established in the church. This person may be given responsibility to contact parents about a parent-teacher meeting, to help organize one or more department outings during the year, to be responsible to see that broken equipment or furnishings are repaired or replaced, etc.

Aids ■ Young people in your church can have a meaningful ministry to young children. A capable young person could work in the department for a month, assisting a teacher and in some cases actually leading a small-group activity.

Specialists ■ These are people with a particular skill which can be used on special occasions: someone who plays a musical instrument can play a few of the children's favorite songs, a skilled storyteller (or reader) can present a Bible story to the department, a carpenter can guide four- and five-year-olds in some simple woodworking activities in the block corner, etc.

CHURCHTIME STAFF

Churchtime is a vital part of the Sunday School's ministry to young children. By providing a second-hour program following Sunday School, a department doubles its time for accomplishing its objectives. The most effective use of this valuable time for young children is to continue the same procedures that were used during the first hour, reinforcing the same Bible learning. Young children need repetition more than they need a total change of pace. Here are four patterns churches have found successful for staffing this important program. In each case, Churchtime personnel need curriculum resources which coordinate with those used by Sunday School teachers in order to build on what occurred the first hour.

1. A Separate, Permanent Staff

Some churches use an entirely new staff for the second hour. The Churchtime staff serves on the same regular basis as the Sunday School teachers. Both staffs meet together for planning. The Churchtime Leader works closely with the Sunday School Department Leader following the direction established in the first hour. Separate staffs work well in churches that have more than one morning worship service.

2. Sunday School Continuity/Rotating Volunteers

The second plan is designed to insure a smooth carry-over between the two hours. One Sunday School teacher serves in both Sunday School and Churchtime for one month. The other teachers are replaced during Churchtime by volunteers who will also serve the full month. The Sunday School teacher serves as leader of the second-hour staff. The next month another teacher and a new group of volunteers take over.

By having the same teacher and volunteers together for the full month, the unit objectives and procedures are easily carried out. The volunteers get satisfaction from seeing a full unit of study carried to completion and they often receive a complete new vision of Early Childhood work. These people then become prime prospects for regular staff positions. There are also those who do have concern and ability but whose circumstances do not allow them to hold a permanent place on the teaching staff. Volunteering to work for a month in Churchtime enables them to serve.

Having the same teachers together for the month benefits the children. They feel secure when familiar people are in charge of the program. This creates fewer discipline problems and more positive learning can take place. Replacing all but one teacher with volunteers for the church hour enables the Sunday School staff to attend church regularly.

3. Permanent Leader/Rotating Volunteers

The third plan combines several features of the first two. A permanent Churchtime Leader serves with a different group of volunteer teachers each month. The Leader attends the Sunday School planning meeting to learn what will be happening the first hour, then briefs that month's volunteers on their assignments to insure a coordinated morning.

The success of this plan depends on the Sunday School staff's willingness to include the Churchtime Leader as part of their team, and the Churchtime Leader's willingness to follow the direction of the Sunday School Department Leader.

Both plans that use rotating volunteers depend heavily on parental cooperation. Usually, the first two volunteers recruited are parents of young children. By participating on this basis occasionally, parents can not only strengthen the church's program, they can also gain new ideas and skills by working with children other than their own alongside an experienced leader. Other groups to contact for volunteers include: high school and college groups, single adults and senior citizens.

4. Rotating Volunteers

This plan is similar to #3 in that volunteers are enlisted to lead Churchtime for a month. It differs from #3 in that there is no permanent leader. This plan works adequately when the church has a pool of capable, experienced people to participate in the program, and/or in smaller churches when group sizes are relatively easy to handle and where children already know most of the people who will be involved. Large churches, or those with large numbers of children in a department, find that sending volunteers into the room without the presence of an experienced leader will result in the volunteers having a less-than-positive experience.

CAUTION: A system of one-Sunday-a-month volunteers has not proven satisfactory in meeting children's educational and emotional needs. Nor do occasional volunteers ever develop a sense of the value of this ministry. The overwhelming attitude in such situations is, "It's a dirty job, but someone's got to do it. I'll take my turn, but don't expect me to like it or try to become good at it."

HOW LARGE A STAFF DO WE NEED?

Every department should always have a minimum of two adults in case of emergency. Departments with eight or less children need a leader and one teacher. Or, the two adults may choose to divide the Teacher and Leader tasks among them, sharing the necessary responsibilities for this size group. Departments with more than eight children need a leader and two or more teachers to maintain the proper teacher/pupil ratio. When a department has more than 15-18 children, a secretary is usually necessary. The age of the children involved determines both the teacher-child ratio and the maximum number of children in a department. Since five-year-olds don't need as much individual attention as babies, more five-year-olds can be in a room than infants.

SUGGESTED MAXIMUM SIZES FOR EARLY CHILDHOOD DEPARTMENTS

(These Maximum Sizes assume the room is large enough to handle that many children at 25-35 feet per child.)

>0-1 year olds—12-15 children
>2-3 year olds—16-20 children
>4-5 year olds—20-24 children

Any departments that exceed these maximums should be divided to create two departments. When these suggested maximums are exceeded, teacher-child relationships suffer, behavior problems increase and learning efficiency decreases.

Because the relationships between teachers and children are

the most important ingredients in a successful Early Childhood department, and because they provide the contact between the church and the home, a proper ratio of teachers to children must be maintained:

TEACHER-CHILD RATIOS

0-1 year olds—1 teacher per 4 children
2-3 year olds—1 teacher per 5 children
4-5 year olds—1 teacher per 6 children

A department with children whose age span covers more than two years should maintain the ratio suggested for the youngest children. The smaller ratio will allow more individual attention to meet the varied needs of each level of development.

HOW CAN WE GET ENOUGH TEACHERS?

Once a church sees the need to maintain proper teacher-child ratios, the question of how to get enough teachers is invariably raised. Which is usually followed with the lament, "Nobody in our church wants to get involved!" When recruiting teachers seems to be a hopeless task, Ephesians 4:4-16 may be encouraging reading.

The Apostle Paul lets us in on the magnificent truth that God has placed within the church all the resources needed to fulfill His mission in the world. Every group of believers in Christ, every congregation, possesses the gifts of ministry. No church needs to wait for someone to come from somewhere else to make the church effective. God has provided your church with the necessary people to get the job done. Your task is to discover and utilize those gifts.

Begin by meeting with the others in your church who share your concern for this ministry: your departmental staff, your division coordinator, the general superintendent and perhaps the pastor. Pray together that God will lead you to the right people, the people that He wants to use. Talk together about the positions needed to be filled and discuss people you know who are suited for the job. Then pray again.

When you have someone in mind, present the name to the responsible church board or officer for approval. The appropriate person should make an appointment to visit in the home of the prospect and:

- Explain the purpose of calling;
- Clearly present the work of the department;
- Show curriculum materials to help the prospect understand the program;
- Tell the person what would be expected in order to be effective and share why you feel he or she would be suited for this work;
- Ask the prospective teacher to observe in the department;
- Then ask the person to pray sincerely about it and make a decision on the basis of what he or she feels God would have him do.

Avoid making the job sound too easy. Teachers who are told there is not much to do usually end up not doing much! After observing, praying and thinking, the prospect should have clearly in mind what lies ahead. The person who declines may still be a prospect for the future as the Lord continues to lead. The person who accepts will be more likely to follow through on this commitment, knowing what to expect.

Notes:

Grouping Young Children Effectively

"Of course Michael should be in the older group! He's very advanced for his age. He's way beyond the baby things they do in the younger class." Michael's mother had fire in her eyes. She was determined that her "uniquely gifted" child should be placed with older children. I was obviously an insensitive clod for doubting the wisdom of this move.

Michael's mother was partly right. Michael was a bright little boy and the teachers in his present department should have been more alert to provide new challenges for him. There is often a tendency for teachers to just keep doing similar activities all year long, not making adjustments for the growing maturity of all the children in the group.

However, the insensitive clod was also right in not wanting to push Michael into an older group. While chronological age is a very imperfect indicator of a child's level of development, most young children are better able to develop at their own pace when they are not pushed to compete with a group of older, more mature children. In Michael's case, he did show advanced dexterity in manipulating puzzles. He was precocious in his ability to write his name and recognize the letters of the alphabet. However, Michael's social skills actually lagged behind those of others in his present department. His speech was very difficult for adults (other than Mom and Dad) to understand. Michael needed time to let his verbal and social development catch up with his academic abilities.

Every church needs a well-thought out policy about grouping and promoting young children. This policy needs to be clearly stated and communicated to parents and teachers. Six major—and sometimes contradictory—guidelines need to be balanced in such a policy:

1. All children and teachers benefit when departments are maintained at similar sizes. An overcrowded group of three-year-olds next door to a nearly empty room of twos is not healthy. This means the church needs to evaluate each year the dividing line between departments. Just because the current cutoff points worked well last year does not mean they will be appropriate this year. (Unless, of course, your church can devise a system to get young couples to evenly space the arrival of new babies.)

2. Children benefit more by being in a smaller group with more personal attention than being in a large, overcrowded group. In the above example, everyone would benefit from placing the younger threes back with the two-year-olds where they could get more individual care and guidance.

3. The oldest Early Childhood department needs to align its policy with the local schools so that children are promoted into the Children's Division when the child is ready to begin first grade. If parents in your area hold younger children (usually boys) out of kindergarten for a year, it is best that those children remain in Early Childhood at church until they actually do enter first grade. Teachers who have six-year-old children in their room for a good part of the year need to be alert for enrichment ideas to keep these children from getting bored with activities

designed for younger children. Consider these general tips:

- Add additional choices of materials to Bible learning activities. For example, increase the number and variety of blocks, the difficulty level of puzzles, the number of paint colors, etc.
- Encourage children to use their developing interest in reading and writing. For example, encourage children to write or dictate comments about an art project, to look at the words of a Bible verse in your Bible, to illustrate the words for a Bible verse or song, etc.
- Give children increased responsibility in caring for equipment, supplies, God's Wonders items, etc.

4. At least one department needs to be designated as a "holding department"—one where children are received from a younger group more than once a year, but are promoted out to the next older group at one time. As a general rule of thumb, the two-year-old department works best as the holding department, since the nature of twos requires very flexible procedures and schedule. The holding department requires a very adaptable staff since this group may be very small at the start of the year and will then grow dramatically as children continue to be promoted in throughout the year.

5. It is best not to promote children (holding department and younger) on their birthdays, but to have periodic promotion days when all those who have reached a designated age (or developmental milestone) are moved to the next department as a group. This enables teachers in both departments to prepare themselves and the child to make the promotion a positive experience.

6. Except in the Babies and Toddlers rooms and in the case of children held out of kindergarten or first grade for a year, age is the safest criterion to use in dividing departments. It is not nec-

essary that the same date be used in dividing all departments. In order to maintain balanced group sizes, it is perfectly reasonable to have one department include a 13-month span while the department next door has only an 11-month span. To avoid confusion, clearly post on the door of each department the specific age range of that group.

Two-Year-Old Department

For Children Whose Second Birthday
Was Between December 15 and August 31

Toddlers need special preparation for their promotion into the two-year-old Sunday School department. As a child approaches the time (preferably two years, three months; or two years, six months) to move on to an older department, arrange an advance visit, with opportunity to meet one new teacher. Talk enthusiastically about specific things the child can do in the new department. Emphasize that the child has now grown big enough to do these things. Encourage parents to recognize the capabilities of their child and the importance of regular Sunday School attendance in these growing and learning years. Expect many toddlers to be reluctant to move, even reverting to crying when parents bring them to their new room. Patient acceptance of their fears about this change will keep any upsets to a minimum.

GROUP SIZES

The young child is a rugged individualist, with little or no sense of being part of a group. Observe a group of children engaged in free play (in a playground, at preschool, in the backyard, etc.). Never will you see twenty five-year-old children organize themselves into any kind of group game. The young child plays alone or alongside a friend with occasional times of interaction with up to three others at a time.

Neither do young children assume that someone speaking to a group is talking to them. Young children are designed for one-to-one interaction with occasional group experiences thrown in for variety. It is not by accident that human mothers do not have litters, but bring their babies into the world one at a time (with occasional multiple births providing added excitement).

The previous chapter dealt with teachers and presented the following Teacher/Child ratios. Extensive experience has shown that these cannot be stretched without impairing relationships, children's behavior, teacher's effectiveness and overall learning efficiency:

> 0-1-year-olds—1 teacher per 4 children;
> 12-14 children maximum
> 2-3-year-olds—1 teacher per 5 children;
> 16-20 children maximum
> 4-5-year-olds—1 teacher per 6 children;
> 20-24 children maximum

Some people question these ratios when preschools and kindergartens consistently operate with 8-30 children per teacher. There are some significant reasons why the larger ratios are not appropriate for a church's once-a-week programs:

1. Large teacher-child ratios in weekday programs are imposed for economic, not educational reasons. The people most closely involved in these programs clearly recognize that children do not receive the quality care or instruction they really need and deserve in large groups. A large percentage of these programs utilize part-time or volunteer aides to reduce the ratios and provide the personal touch the child needs.

2. Reputable weekday programs are staffed by professionally trained and supervised personnel. Most once-a-week church ministries are staffed and supervised by volunteers who often

have very minimal time for training and preparation. Expecting these volunteers to work with the same group sizes as professionals is a good way to kill off a lot of volunteers.

3. Weekday programs have the children for 2 ½ hours or more per day, two to five days per week. The teacher is able to move among the children at a relaxed pace and be sure that each one gets some personal attention at some time during every week. The one-hour programs of the church do not allow the teacher time to have some eyeball-to-eyeball, nose-to-nose interaction with every child if the above ratios are exceeded.

4. Relationships between teachers and children are the most powerful dimension of a Sunday School or Churchtime session. While it may be possible to entertain or inform or "handle" a large group of young children, the church is not in the handling business. The church is called to love one another—and young children can only be loved on a one-to-one basis.

HOW MANY DEPARTMENTS DO WE NEED?

Once a church knows how many teachers it needs for the number of children that attend—and what the maximum department sizes should be for each age level, it is time to decide how many departments are needed. The answer may get complicated by several factors. For instance, since young children need 25-35 square feet of space, many rooms may not be large enough to accommodate the maximum group sizes. Thus, a church with rooms smaller than 800 square feet would need more departments with fewer children each than a church with larger rooms.

Assuming that a church has (1) adequate space to accommodate maximum group sizes; and (2) approximately the same number of children in each age group, the following chart indicates the number of departments—and staff—needed as attendance grows.

GROUPING CHILDREN IN THE EARLY CHILDHOOD DIVISION

...when the attendance numbers less than:

5	30	50	80	110	220
You need **1** department of children...	You need **2** departments of children...	You need **3** departments of children...	You need **5** departments of children...	You need **6** departments of children...	You need **12** departments of children...
			Babies	Babies	Babies
	0–1 years	0–1 years	Toddlers	Toddlers	Toddlers
0–5 years			2's	2's	2's 2's
		2–3 years	3's	3's	3's 3's
	2–5 years			4's	4's 4's
		4–5 years	4–5 years	5's	5's 5's
...with 1 department leader and 1 teacher	...with 2 department leaders, 2–5 teachers	...with 3 department leaders, 3–10 teachers	...with 5 department leaders, 5–16 teachers	...with 6 department leaders, 6–22 teachers	...with 12 department leaders, 12–44 teachers

If the total number of children attending is less than 30, read Section 1.

If the total number of children attending is between 30 and 49, read Section 2.

If the total number of children attending is between 50 and 79, read Section 3.

If the total number of children attending is 80 or over, read Section 4.

A SAMPLE CHART FOR EVALUATING YOUR PRESENT SITUATION

Department	No. of Dept. Leaders	No. of Teachers	No. of Children	Teacher/ Children Ratio

While we plan for the present, it also helps to look toward the future. If you anticipate an increased attendance because of outreach programs within the next few years, refer to the section following the one recommended for your present attendance.

Section 1:

Churches with less than 30 children in attendance between the ages of birth and five should plan two Early Childhood departments with the babies and toddlers grouped together in one department and the rest in another.

If there are five or less children it may be temporarily necessary for these children to be in the same room as the infants and toddlers. Be sure babies and toddlers have a safe area of their own. One or two simple learning activities should be included for the older group during the morning.

A teacher should take the threes, fours and fives sometime during the morning to a quiet area of the room and present the Bible story. Include a few songs and finger fun. The two-year-olds and toddlers may gradually join the group, especially during the songs and finger fun.

Section 2:

Churches with 30 to 49 children need three Early Childhood departments. Once total attendance exceeds 30 and is distributed evenly between the age groups, a department for babies and toddlers, a department for twos and threes and a department for fours and fives will provide effectively for all children. A church with a large number of babies and toddlers will find it helpful to have babies up to 18 months in one room, children up to three and a half years in the second and older threes in with the fours and fives.

Section 3:

Churches with a total attendance of 50 to 79 children between the ages of birth and five will need four or five Early Childhood departments. Again department divisions should be determined to provide balanced group sizes. The young child's need to be in a group where individual needs can be met should take precedence over adult desires to have uniform age division.

Section 4:

If your church has an attendance of 80 or more children between the ages of birth and five, you need a minimum of six Early Childhood departments.

A Room for Learning

Young Isaac learned his greatest lesson on a mountainside when Abraham, his father, built a crude altar of stones. The boy Samuel encountered God in the middle of the night while in bed. Jonah discovered God's purposes while he was on a boat in a storm, while in the belly of a giant fish and while sitting in the sun outside the city of Nineveh. Jesus taught many of His most vivid truths while near the shore of a lake and while walking along dusty roads.

What kind of place do the young children in your church need to help them learn important truths about God? Obviously, insights about God may come to a person in any setting. God is never limited by our physical surroundings. However, God did create young children with certain physical and learning characteristics which we need to take into careful consideration when planning the place we want to teach them.

THE LEARNING ENVIRONMENT

Young children work, play and learn with their whole bodies. They require rooms equipped for action. Open space, child-sized equipment, and safe, interesting materials make children feel their room at church is a good place to be. When children feel this way, teachers can effectively accomplish their Bible teaching ministry.

Space Requirements

Young children need to move, and movement requires space. Each child needs a minimum of 25 to 35 square feet (7.5 to 10.5 sq. m) of space. Multiply the number of children in your room by

35 (or 10.5). Your answer represents the number of square feet (or meters) your room should contain. To determine how many children your present room can adequately handle, first measure the length and width of your room. Multiply these two measurements. Divide the answer by 35 (or 10.5). What is the child capacity of your room? How does this number compare with your attendance?

Rectangular-shaped rooms (about three-fourths as wide as they are long) provide more flexibility in room arrangements than a square or a long, narrow one.

It is recommended that all Early Childhood rooms have at least eight hundred to one thousand square feet.

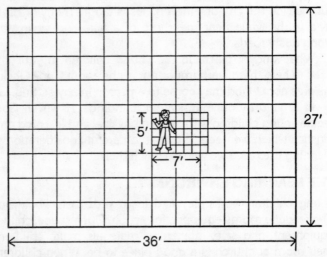

The idea of 25 to 35 square feet per person can be understood as an area 5x7 feet for each child. (Or 7.5 to 10.5 sq. m. per person is an area 1.5x2.1 m. for each child.)

This size room will accommodate the maximum attendance for five-year-old children, and will allow needed extra space per child should the rooms be used for younger groups.

The Room Itself

The ideal *location* for all Early Childhood departments is at ground level, with quick and easy access to a safe outside area. Rooms on the first floor allow efficient safety precautions as well as convenience for parents. When teachers take children out of doors, they can do so with a minimum of confusion.

Select a *floor covering* that is durable and easy to clean. Vinyl tile in a subdued pattern is very satisfactory. Washable carpeting provides a quiet, relaxed atmosphere and is well worth considering. A rug on which children sit for group activities should be provided if the room has a hard, cold floor. The floor should be thoroughly cleaned after each session, especially in rooms for babies, toddlers and twos.

Acoustical *ceilings* help deaden sounds; *walls* also should be insulated to block sound and be furnished with some sound-absorbing materials (bulletin boards, etc.). *Windows* of clear glass, with the bottom sill two feet (60 cm) from the floor, provide children with a backdrop of God's Wonders. No window covering is usually necessary except to reduce glare and provide insulation.

Toilet facilities that immediately adjoin each room are desirable for children over two, and essential for babies and toddlers. A sink and child-level drinking fountain in the department are also good investments. When a room has no sink, plastic dishpans and pitchers can be used for activities requiring water.

Electrical outlets equipped with safety plugs and out of children's reach should be provided on each wall to avoid the hazards of extension cords.

Active young children need a *room temperature* between 68 and 70 degrees Fahrenheit (or 21 degrees Celsius). A thermometer hung about three feet (90 cm) from the floor monitors temperature at the children's level. Radiators must be covered for safety. Adequate ventilation is also a must, for a room of active children can get stuffy very easily, thus making children restless and uncomfortable. Check for drafts from doors and windows.

Lighting should be even and without glare in all parts of the room. Soft pastel wall colors help to create a warm, cheery atmosphere—so vital to the welfare of young children. To brighten rooms which are gloomy on darker days, use a soft yellow or pink wall color. To reduce glare in a sunny room, select a pale blue or green color. Bright colors can be added as highlights, but should not overpower bulletin board displays and other teaching tools.

Display and Storage Equipment

Bulletin board space is desirable for visualizing the theme for a unit of lessons and for displaying decorations children help prepare and arrange. One large bulletin board hung 18 inches (45 cm) from the floor should be placed as a backdrop in the area where children gather for Together Time. Other boards may be placed in activity areas to display related materials. Avoid cluttering the walls with unnecessary decorations. Only pictures related to the unit of study and children's current art work should be displayed. A "Parents' Board" should be mounted in the hallway and kept up to date with information related to the current unit.

To renew unsightly bulletin boards, cover the entire surface with colorful burlap, other fabric or colored paper.

Easels are not recommended for Early Childhood rooms as they take up floor space and seem to invite children to crawl around underneath them. Small *flannel boards* that can be held on a teacher's lap are effective for displaying visual aids to a group, and they can easily be put away when not in use.

Ample *storage space* in each department is necessary. Much money is wasted when curriculum materials are not systematically stored, when scissors are lost and when markers are not put away. For teacher's materials, build cabinets mounted about 50 inches (125 cm) from the floor. This installation frees the floor space below the cabinets, making more room for children's learning activities.

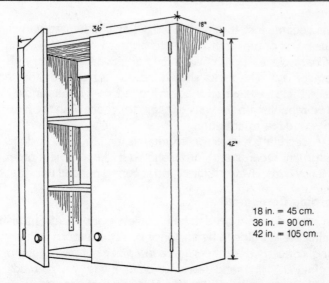

18 in. = 45 cm.
36 in. = 90 cm.
42 in. = 105 cm.

For displaying and storing children's materials and equipment, low, open shelves have proven most successful. Children can see what materials are available, can help themselves, and then can return material to the shelves.

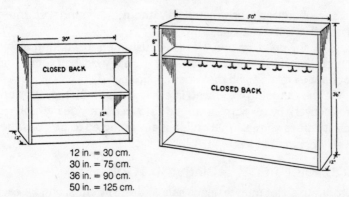

12 in. = 30 cm.
30 in. = 75 cm.
36 in. = 90 cm.
50 in. = 125 cm.

Avoid throwing things in a bin. A box or a bin with materials piled in haphazardly is perhaps the poorest kind of storage unit. Children see chaos rather than an orderly display of materials;

items become lost, torn and soiled. Often children want to climb inside a box or bin, creating a safety hazard.

Coatracks for both children and adults are necessary pieces of equipment. The racks should include a place to store hats, purses, Bibles, etc. When space is limited, coat hooks and a shelf can be mounted on the wall, either in the room or in the hall outside your department door.

A *secretary's desk or counter* is helpful at the door. All department records and forms should be kept in neat order for efficiency in receiving children and securing needed information.

Learning Equipment

Your room does not need to be completely or perfectly furnished for effective learning to begin. Once you staff a room with several loving, concerned teachers and a few pieces of basic equipment for children's firsthand learning experiences, you're ready for action! Organize furnishings to form several centers or areas. Furnish each area to facilitate the special learning that will take place there. This kind of arrangement is worth considering for several reasons:

1. Children can use materials without interfering with those involved in other activities.

2. A shy child, or one who is accustomed to working alone, can participate in a small area with a clearly defined focus and not have to relate to all the other children.

3 The outgoing child who is easily overstimulated can work productively in a room arranged into centers. Clearly defined activity areas suggest that children are expected to be constructively occupied in learning.

EQUIPMENT FOR BABIES AND TODDLERS

A room used for infants needs safe and sturdy cribs, one for each baby. Be cautious about stacking cribs. Building committees tend to view them as the solution to crowded nurseries, but they can easily result in trying to squeeze too many infants in too small a space. In addition, the close proximity of these cribs can contribute to the spread of illness among babies. Also consider the height of the mattress and avoid forcing nursery teachers to bend or stretch uncomfortably to pick up a child.

One or two playpens of lightweight, easy-to-clean nylon are also needed, as well as one or two adult rocking chairs, changing tables, infant swing and diaper bag storage out of the child's reach.

Clean sheets for each crib each week are a must; also soft slippers for the teachers to wear in the room. (High heels are dangerous with creeping babies.) If teachers wear smocks, these must be washed after each session. Warm crib covers, disposable diapers and wastebaskets with liners are also necessary.

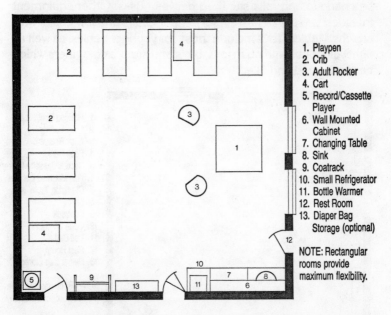

1. Playpen
2. Crib
3. Adult Rocker
4. Cart
5. Record/Cassette Player
6. Wall Mounted Cabinet
7. Changing Table
8. Sink
9. Coatrack
10. Small Refrigerator
11. Bottle Warmer
12. Rest Room
13. Diaper Bag Storage (optional)

NOTE: Rectangular rooms provide maximum flexibility.

Near the changing table or on shelves out of the child's reach, keep a dispenser of wet towels, plus tissues, plastic bags, cotton balls and baby oil. Use plastic or paper containers rather than glass. Place the baby on a plastic or vinyl surface for changing, then wrap the soiled diaper in a plastic bag. Carefully wipe the changing surface with a sterilizing solution after each use. Provide washable cuddle and squeeze toys, rattles, books and simple colorful pictures. Check all toys regularly to be sure they are in safe condition, with no parts that could be swallowed. Toys, bed rails and playpen rails need to be sterilized after each use. Check with your druggist about a safe, effective sterilizing solution.

A room for babies who are crawling does not require a crib for every child, since some will prefer to be in a playpen, on the floor or on a teacher's lap for much of the session. When a crib is used by more than one child during the morning, sheets must be changed and rails sterilized between uses. Other equipment includes: two playpens, several jumper chairs and low chairs with attached tables. Toys include those for younger babies, as well as lightweight pull and push toys, balls and simple containers which can be nested and filled.

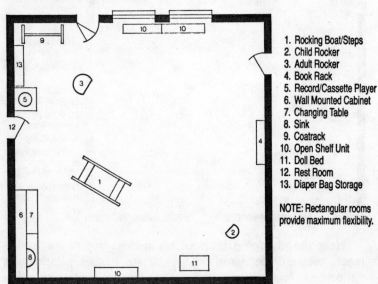

1. Rocking Boat/Steps
2. Child Rocker
3. Adult Rocker
4. Book Rack
5. Record/Cassette Player
6. Wall Mounted Cabinet
7. Changing Table
8. Sink
9. Coatrack
10. Open Shelf Unit
11. Doll Bed
12. Rest Room
13. Diaper Bag Storage

NOTE: Rectangular rooms provide maximum flexibility.

An important safety precaution is to separate toddlers completely from the babies either by having separate rooms or by substantial room dividers. Allowing toddlers to play near infants is an invitation to have a baby get poked, pinched, hit or stepped on.

The room needs: a few cribs, a changing table, an adult rocking chair, one child-size table (chairs are optional), a doll bed (sturdy enough for children to climb into) and blankets, a rocking boat/climbing steps unit and cardboard or fabric blocks. Toys to add to the toddler room include several sturdy ride-on toys, stacking and nesting toys, and several dolls with molded plastic heads.

ROCKING BOAT

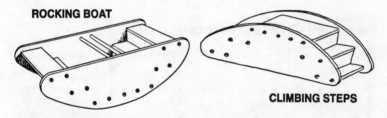

CLIMBING STEPS

(The rocking boat is built so that, when turned upside down, it becomes a set of climbing steps.)

EQUIPMENT FOR TWOS THROUGH FIVES

Rooms for children over two look very different from those for babies and toddlers. Areas of the room are more clearly defined, specialized equipment and furniture have been introduced, and a wider variety of learning materials are available. However, the rooms still need to have considerable open space.

Chairs should be from 10-14 inches (25-35 cm) from the floor depending on the height of the children using them. Select chairs that are sturdy and not easily tipped over, but light enough for children to move. No adult-sized chairs are needed (except for secretary) since adults should work at the child's eye level. To avoid the confusion of moving chairs have children sit on the rug for Together Time. The seating area on the floor can be defined with masking tape placed in a semicircle. "Sit on the line" is an easier instruction for children to follow than "make a circle." When space is limited, eliminate unnecessary chairs or other furniture.

Tables should be 18-22 inches (45-55 cm) high, 10 inches (25 cm) higher than the chairs. The tabletop, durable and washable, should be approximately 30×48 inches (75x120 cm). Avoid large tables that seat more than six. Select tables that allow the teacher to be within arm's reach of all children. Round tables have the advantages of being "friendly" and of having no corners. They are more expensive than rectangular tables which are more efficient work areas, especially for art projects.

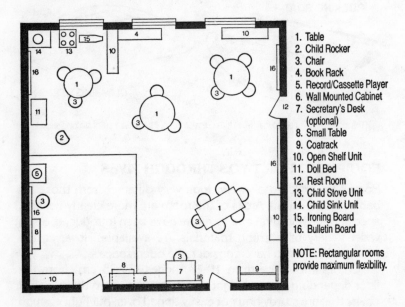

1. Table
2. Child Rocker
3. Chair
4. Book Rack
5. Record/Cassette Player
6. Wall Mounted Cabinet
7. Secretary's Desk (optional)
8. Small Table
9. Coatrack
10. Open Shelf Unit
11. Doll Bed
12. Rest Room
13. Child Stove Unit
14. Child Sink Unit
15. Ironing Board
16. Bulletin Board

NOTE: Rectangular rooms provide maximum flexibility.

Securing Needed Equipment

Because limited budgets often force department leaders to acquire equipment one piece at a time, it is vital that a well-thought-out set of priorities be established so that the most necessary things are purchased first.

In selecting equipment, it is often wiser to buy a few well-made items than many less expensive and less durable ones. Equipment of superior quality is well worth the investment in terms of years of hard wear.

Many times churches become the recipients of donated cast-offs. These materials may have been suitable for home play, but frequently are not appropriate in a Sunday School setting. Thank the donor, saying, "We'll look it over and pass it on to other children if it is not something the children are able to use in this setting." You may give unneeded donations to an organization which repairs toys for reuse by charitable groups. When asking for donated items, be very specific in describing the materials needed.

Specific materials and equipment required for each area of the room are discussed in detail when each activity is described in chapter 11, "Active Learning for Active Children."

BASIC FURNISHINGS AND EQUIPMENT FOR BABIES AND TODDLERS

■ Babies

Quiet Experiences

Books/Pictures ● Picture books of fabric or cardboard (washable)
   ● Pictures
mounted on cardboard, covered with clear adhesive paper.

God's Wonders ● Nature materials (cut flowers, plants, fish)
   ● Unbreakable mirror

Music ● Record player/cassette player ● Assortment of recordings (lullabies,
simple songs)

Feeding/Rest/Changing ● Bottle warmer ● Refrigerator ● Baby schedule card ● Changing table or carts ● Disposable diapers ● Soft paper towels, tissues, cotton balls ● Baby oil ● Sterilizing solution
   ● Blankets, sheets

Active Experiences

Dolls ● Dolls with rubber molded heads ● Washable squeeze toys
● Washable cuddle toys

Toys ● Rattles ● Crib mobile ● Balls (5″ to 9″—12.5 × 22.5 cm diameter)
● Washable fabric blocks ● Baby exerciser ● Clutch ball ● Texture ball

General Equipment

Cribs (hospital type) ● Playpen (nylon mesh) ● Blankets, sheets ● Adult rockers (2) ● Wall supply cabinets ● Plastic wastebasket ● Adult coatrack ● Toilet and sink

■ Toddlers

Quiet Experiences

Books/Pictures ● Picture books of fabric or cardboard (washable)
● Pictures mounted on cardboard, covered with clear adhesive paper

God's Wonders ● Nature materials (cut flowers, plants, fish, small animals)
Magnifying glass ● Unbreakable mirror

Music ● Record player/cassette player ● Assortment of recordings of activity songs, lullabies (simple songs)

Feeding/Rest/Changing ● Paper cups, napkins ● Changing table
● Disposable diapers ● Soft paper towels, tissues, cotton balls ● Baby oil ● Sterilizing solution ● Blankets, sheets

Active Experiences

Dolls ● Dolls with plastic molded heads ● Washable squeeze toys
● Washable cuddle toys ● Doll bed (28″ × 14″ × 11″—70 × 35 × 27.5 cm) ● Doll blankets ● Plastic telephones ● Soft plastic dishes
● Small round table (optional)

Toys ● Push and pull toys ● Fill and dump toys ● Nesting and stacking puzzles ● Wooden jigsaw puzzles (3-4 pieces) ● Large cardboard blocks ● Balls (5″ × 9″—12.5 to 22.5 cm diameter) ● Open shelf for storage ● Rocking boat/Climbing steps ● Ride on toys

General Equipment

Adult rocker ● Wall supply cabinets ● Plastic wastebasket ● Coatracks (adult and child) ● Toilet and sink

BASIC FURNISHINGS AND EQUIPMENT FOR 2s and 3s
(See Chapter 11 for teaching tips on how to use these Bible Learning
Activity materials.)

Activity Areas	Furniture	Equipment and Materials
Home Living	Cabinet sink unit (24″—60 cm high work surface) Stove (24″—60 cm high) Table (30″ × 48—75 × 120 cm surface or round w/ 40″—100 cm diameter, 20″—50 cm high) 4-6 chairs (10″—25 cm high) Doll bed (28″ × 14″ × 11— 70 × 35 × 27.5 cm) Rocking chair, child-sized Ironing board	Bible with pictures Safe plastic dishes Doctor play materials Dolls, rubber molded head Dress-up clothes (male & female) Two plastic telephones Doll bedding
Art	Bible with pictures Table (30″ × 48″—75 × 120 cm surface 20″—50 cm high) 4-6 (10″—25 cm high) Small cothes drying rack (for wet paintings) Open shelves with closed back (12″—30 cm deep)	Long-handled paintbrushes, ¾″ bristles Paste, glue Large newsprint sheets Salt/flour dough or Play Doh Tempera, assorted colors Smocks or aprons Large crayons Sponges
Books	Book rack (27″ × 67.5 cm high)	Bible with pictures Books recommended in Teacher's Manual
God's Wonders	Low, open shelves with closed back (12″—30 cm deep)	Bible with pictures Nature materials (plants, aquarium, magnifying glass)

Blocks	Open shelves with closed back (12"—30 cm deep) Balance beam (4" to 6"—10 to 15 cm wide)	Bible with pictures Blocks (large cardboard for twos, wooden for threes) Sturdy wooden trucks, cars, etc. Block accessories (people, animals, etc.) Balls (7" to 9"—17.5 to 22.5 cm diameter)
Puzzles	Puzzle rack Table (30" × 48"—75 × 120 cm) surface or round w/ 40"—100 cm diameter, (20"—50 cm high) 4-6 chairs (10"—25 cm high)	Bible with pictures Wooden puzzles (3-12 pieces) Gadget board Large wooden beads Felt boards
Music/ Worship	Record player/cassette player Autoharp	Bible with pictures Pictures as recommended in Teacher's Manual Recordings listed in Teacher's Manual *Little Ones Sing* songbook *Fun-to-Sing* songbook and cassette
Miscellaneous	2 wall supply cabinets (50"—125 cm from floor) Coatracks for adults and children Secretary's desk Toilets Sink or plastic dishpans	Record forms Sterilizing solution Plastic wastebasket

BASIC FURNISHINGS AND EQUIPMENT FOR 4s and 5s
(See Chapter 11 for teaching tips on how to use these Bible Learning
    Activity materials.)

Activity Areas	Furniture	Equipment and Materials
Home Living	Cabinet sink unit (24"—60 cm high work surface)	Bible with pictures
	Stove (24"—60 cm high)	Soft plastic dishes
	Table (30"×48"—75×120 cm surface or round w/ 40"—100 cm diameter, 22"—55 cm high)	Doctor play materials
		Dolls (10" to 20"—25 to 50 cm long)
		Two plastic telephones
	4-6 chairs (12"—30 cm high)	Cleaning materials, child-sized (mop, broom, dustpan)
	Doll bed (28"×14"×11"—70×35×27.5 cm)	Cooking utensils, child-sized
	Rocking chair, child-sized	Doll bedding
	Chest of drawers (24"—60 cm high)	Dress-up clothes (male & female)
	Ironing board	
Art	Table (30"×48"—75×120 cm surface or round w/ 40"—100 cm diameter, 22"—55 cm high)	Bible with pictures
		Long-handled brushes, ¾"—1.9 cm bristles
	4-6 chairs (12"—30 cm high)	Construction paper
		Large crayons
	Small clothes drying rack (for wet paintings)	Finger paints
		Manila paper, large sheets
	Open shelves with closed back (12"—30 cm deep)	Newsprint, large sheets
		Smocks
		Paste, white glue, glue sticks
		Salt/flour dough or clay
		Tempera, assorted colors
		Scissors (blunt tip)

Books	Book rack (33"—82.5 cm high) Table (30" × 48"—75 × 120 cm surface or round w/ 40"—100 cm diameter, 22"—55 cm high) 4 chairs (12"—30 cm high)	Bible with pictures Books recommended in Teacher's Manual
God's Wonders	Low open shelves with closed back (12"—30 cm deep)	Bible with pictures Nature materials (plants, acquarium, magnifying glass, magnet, etc.)
Blocks	Open shelves with closed back (12"—30 cm deep)	Bible with pictures Sturdy wooden trucks, cars, etc. Blocks (wooden unit) Block accessories (people, animals, etc.)
Puzzle	Puzzle rack Table (24" × 36"—60 × 90 cm surface or round w/ 40"—100 cm diameter, 22"—55 cm high)	Bible with pictures Wooden puzzles (10+ pieces) Gadget board Felt boards
Music/ Worship	Record player/cassette player Autoharp	Bible with pictures Rhythm instruments Recordings, as recommended in Teacher's Manual *Little Ones Sing* songbook *Fun-to-Sing* songbook and cassette

Miscellaneous	2 wall supply cabinets (50″—125 cm from floor)	Record forms
		Plastic wastebasket
	Bulletin boards (child's eye level)	
	Coatracks	
	Secretary's desk	
	Toilets	
	Sink or plastic dishpans	

An Early Childhood department provides a variety of simultaneous activities from which each child is free to choose.

A Good Session for the Young Child

There are 168 hours in every week. The young child spends those hours in a wide variety of activities, each of which has an impact in forming the developing child. Time is spent with family members, at preschool, with a baby sitter, playing with friends, watching television, looking at books, running, jumping, pretending, drawing, imitating, daydreaming, exploring—the list is enough to make any adult tired!

Out of all those busy hours in the week, the child will spend only one or two of them with you. Should the child be absent for a session or two, your impact on that child is greatly reduced. The little time you and the child are together must be used effectively to produce effective, long-lasting learning.

SUNDAY MORNING FOR BABIES AND TODDLERS

■ Babies

Welcome
- [ ] Speak warmly and softly to each baby.
- [ ] Place baby in crib with toy.
- [ ] Have parents complete feeding/sleeping schedule card or check card on file.
- [ ] Have parents label all personal belongings (if not already done).
- [ ] Attach identification tags to diaper bag; put in designated place.
- [ ] Be alert for symptoms of illness. Do not admit baby with signs of cold or other sickness.
- [ ] Keep parents and older children outside room.

During Session

- ☐ Follow instructions on each baby's feeding/sleeping schedule card.
- ☐ Talk and sing softly to babies while feeding and diapering.
- ☐ Wash hands thoroughly after diapering each baby.
- ☐ Cuddle and rock each baby; play gently.
- ☐ Provide changes of toys for each baby.
- ☐ Show book and/or picture; talk about each item.
- ☐ Show God's Wonders items; talk about each one.
- ☐ Re-sterilize all toys after use.
- ☐ Keep each baby's belongings in designated place.
- ☐ Cuddle and rock crying babies.

Departure

- ☐ Release baby only to parents or other adult designated by parents.
- ☐ Describe baby's morning to parents, especially any deviations from schedule.
- ☐ Have parents double-check baby's belongings.
- ☐ File feeding/sleeping card.
- ☐ Remove sheets from cribs.
- ☐ Wash toys and put away.
- ☐ Leave room in order.

■ Toddlers

Welcome

- ☐ Speak warmly and softly to each child, stooping to child's eye level.
- ☐ Help child get involved with learning materials or with another teacher. Comfort if crying.
- ☐ Have parents label all personal belongings if not already done.
- ☐ Attach identification tag to diaper bag; put in designated place.
- ☐ Be alert for symptoms of illness. Do not admit child showing signs of cold or other sickness.

☐ Keep parents and older children outside room.

During Session
☐ Talk and sing softly to children in all activities.
☐ Play gently and lovingly with each child; cuddle child when he or she desires.
☐ Provide duplicate toy in case of conflict.
☐ Show books and pictures; talk about each item.
☐ Show God's Wonders items; talk about each one.
☐ Participate with child in doll play.
☐ Help as needed in working puzzles.
☐ Assist with use of rocking boat/climbing steps.
☐ Participate in block building.
☐ Talk lovingly while changing diaper. Wash hands.
☐ Comfort crying child; provide favorite activity.

Departure
☐ Release child only to parents or other adult designated by parents.
☐ Describe child's morning to parents; specifically recount positive achievements.
☐ Have parents double-check child's belongings.
☐ Wash toys thoroughly and put away.
☐ Leave room in order.

SUNDAY MORNING SCHEDULE FOR YOUNG CHILDREN

It makes no difference to the young child what time is announced as the "official" beginning of Sunday School. As far as the child is concerned, Sunday School starts the moment he or she walks in the door. Whether the child enters enthusiastically or shyly, eagerly or reluctantly, the first few moments will set the tone for the rest of the session.

Step 1—Bible Learning Activities

Each child's arrival deserves a warm, personal greeting and the opportunity to immediately begin doing something interesting and enjoyable. The only way you can provide this essential touch for each child is to be in the room at least 15 minutes before the first child arrives. Do your preparing and organizing of materials ahead of time so that you are ready to focus on the individual needs and interests of each child.

Take a look around the room and observe what children will see as they enter:

- Are all unneeded items out of the way to reduce clutter and distractions?
- Are all this session's equipment and materials placed where children can see and reach them easily?
- Is the Department Leader, Secretary or a Teacher at the door, ready to welcome each child personally?
- Are the other teachers in an activity area, prepared to help children learn? (Remember, the number of activities you can offer at one time is determined by the number of teachers—one activity per teacher.)

Here comes the first child. The leader bends down to welcome him by name. "Adam, I'm so glad to see you. We have lots of things for you to do today!" While talking with the child, the leader makes a quick observation of the child's health status. Any signs of fever or cold warrant not admitting the child in order to protect the other children. After a friendly but brief word to the parents, Adam is brought into the room.

He may need a bit of help with his coat. However, the leader wisely lets the child do as much for himself as possible. Adam finds his own name tag (he's four). Next he visits the Love Gift Center where the leader says, "We bring our love gifts because we love God." Adam is now ready to choose the activity he wants to explore first. The leader may explain the options available, but no effort is made to force a child to participate against his will.

As the other children arrive the same procedure continues. Teachers remain at their assigned areas whether or not children have begun working at that activity. The leader does seek to guide children to the less crowded areas. If an activity is so popular not everyone who desires can participate, make a list of those who want to do it and assure them you will let them know as soon as there is room. Then guide them to try another activity in the meantime.

Babies and Toddlers

If Adam were under two years old the procedures would be much the same. The parents would check his file card to see if eating and sleeping information is still current. The leader would check to be sure the diaper bag is properly marked and stored. Then Adam would begin his morning with a favorite toy—either in a crib, a playpen or on the floor, depending on his age. The rest of the morning for a baby or toddler involves individual interaction with teachers in play, conversation, singing, feeding and resting.

Why begin the session with a choice of activities? There are four main reasons:

1. Children do not all arrive at the same time. If the session began with large group time, the constant interruption of children arriving would greatly distract the group's attention.

2. Few children come to Sunday School mentally and physically ready to sit quietly. It's too early in the day for that. They are filled with energy and vitality; they want something to do! Bible Learning Activities provide a purposeful and acceptable means of releasing this energy.

3. The activities that teachers provide are prepared to capture children's interest and to naturally guide their thinking toward the learning objective for the day. As the child begins playing with clay, the teacher at that table may say, "The clay feels good, doesn't it? The Bible says that God gives us all good things."

4. Even young children prefer to make their own choices. A multitude of discipline problems can be avoided by allowing a child to select from among several possibilities, rather than telling him or her to do what everyone else is doing. Giving a child a choice from among appropriate options helps in learning to

make decisions and accept responsibility. It also shows that you have respect for the child as a person.

Throughout Bible Learning Activity time, children are allowed to move freely to whatever activity they desire. When they tire of one activity, they move to another. This freedom of movement creates a relaxed atmosphere that both teachers and children enjoy. Children respond best when allowed to work at their own pace at activities of their own choice. Teachers are then able to concentrate on guiding their activities, with less need for trying to cajole a reluctant child into doing something in which the child has little interest.

Some observers ask, "When do the children stop playing and start learning?" Play is the way God planned for small children to do most of their learning. The child who builds with blocks, paints a picture, lives out real experiences in the Home Living area, etc., is learning how to relate to other children. Play is how a child discovers that church people are truly concerned about the important things in daily life. As a teacher casually asks questions and engages the child in conversation, the child begins thinking about the lesson concepts for that morning. In the midst of this guided play there are repeated opportunities to share a Bible thought, to sing a song or even tell the Bible story. Because this firsthand learning is so important to young children, half or more of the Sunday School session is spent in these activities.

In order to keep the flow of children smooth and pleasant, it is very helpful for the leader to be free to guide a child into new activities: "Suki, if you're tired of building with blocks, you could walk over to the art table to see what's happening there." The leader also moves from group to group, quietly assisting where needed. Behavior challenges, such as crying children, can be handled by the leader, thus allowing teachers to focus on the group in their area. The leader is also able to observe each teacher at work, which is essential for the leader to be able to encourage teachers in specific ways to improve.

Bible Learning Activity time concludes when the leader indicates with a signal (a chord on the Autoharp, a song about cleaning up, flicking the lights) that it is time to clean up. Children learn responsibility and the importance of helping when they participate in cleanup. Cleanup tasks also help develop the child's sense of accomplishment as well as fostering respect for the room. Open shelves that are easily accessible make cleanup easy and pleasant for the children. Clearly marked containers aid children—and teachers—in getting materials into the right places. The children come to the circle as they complete cleanup tasks. The leader is already at the circle leading activity songs or finger fun as the children join together.

An Early Childhood department provides a variety of simultaneous activities
from which each child is free to choose.

Additional Bible Learning Activity information, including valuable teaching tips, can be found in Chapter 11, "Active Learning for Active Children."

Step 2—Together Time

The second major time block in the schedule brings all the children and teachers together in a semicircle on the rug. There are several reasons for having a large group time:

1. Bringing everyone together provides opportunities for the

leader to reinforce the Bible learning that took place during Bible Learning Activities. Conversation, songs, finger fun, an activity and prayer all serve to call attention to the lesson focus.

2. Simple games and songs also help children become aware of each other. When leader begins to sing "I have a good friend, _____ is his name," attention is focused on individual children and teachers in the group. By asking the group, "Who is not here today?" or leading them in prayer for a child who is ill, the leader is building a concern for others.

3. The large group also allows participation in activities that might be disruptive if done by only a few. Singing, marching and finger play may be done in small groups, but when everyone is participating there is no worry about disturbing those involved in another activity.

4. The large group experience gives the Department Leader a chance for in-service teacher training. As teachers observe the leader talking with children and involving them in activities, they can improve their own teaching techniques.

5. Finally, the large group time changes the pace of the morning. Children will tire less readily when they are given a change of activity. Doing something new always sparks interest.

These tips are important for an effective Together Time:

1. Avoid Dead Time. Start an activity song or finger fun with the first few arrivers and keep something going until everyone is in place. Waiting for the group to gather is simply inviting problems.

2. Change Pace and Position. Plan Together Time to include some quiet (prayer, Bible verse conversation) and some active (song, finger fun, game) events. At times, have children stand and move. Remember, a child's brief attention span gets even briefer in a large group where the child is expected to sit and listen.

3. Be Flexible. Be willing to switch your plans to fit the way things are going. Be ready to end or omit something if children are restless or take more time on something which "clicks."

4. Have Something Extra Ready. An activity song or game can quickly recapture interest. A cassette tape of interesting sounds always triggers curiosity. A finger fun poem with simple actions allows wiggly bodies to move appropriately.

5. Teachers Participate. Together Time is not when teachers get ready for their Bible story or put away Bible Learning Activity materials. Teachers are needed sitting alongside the children to set positive examples of what children are to do. And teachers can quietly deal with any disruptive behavior, allowing the leader to focus on the learning procedures. Often, just a teacher's hand on a child's shoulder will stop disruptive behavior.

6. Emphasize the Positive. Give recognition to the children who come quickly to the circle, who show they are ready to learn, who respond correctly to an instruction. Sometimes in a large group, it is the child who disrupts who is noticed, a practice which simply encourages more disruptive efforts to gain attention. Two of the most positive things the leader can do to draw children's interest are to use children's names and to establish eye contact with them.

7. Guide Children's Participation. A large group (any gathering of more than six children) requires some specialized procedures to enable children to participate without having the time degenerate into chaos. One essential large group procedure is to establish a signal for children to use when they wish to speak: "When I ask a question, if you know the answer, put your thumb on your knee." The signal should be silent and stationary, so eager children do not get themselves over-stimulated by waving arms in attempts to gain attention. In using a signal, it is important to emphasize the specific procedures you want the children to follow: "I am calling on children who are being very quiet and who have their thumbs on their knees." It is not necessary to call on the first child to respond, but it is important to recognize those who show they know the answer: "Brandon has his thumb on his knee. Good. And Jonathan knows the answer, too. Katie, you can tell us the answer." Using a signal in this way not only helps control the group from all talking at once, it allows you to give slower, younger and shyer children a chance to participate.

Are all young children ready for group time? By the time a child is past three, a 7- to 10-minute group time is effective for most. Two-year-olds and even some toddlers can participate in group time if it is kept very brief. They should not be required to participate in group activities. Some will participate eagerly; some will observe from the sidelines; others will ignore the group completely.

Step 3—Bible Story/Activity Time

Our objective in telling Bible stories to small children is not primarily for them to remember the details of events. It is to allow the biblical material to speak to the child about the everyday business of living.

Bible Learning Activity time at the start of the session provides many opportunities to tell a Bible story. What could be more natural than during the investigation of God's Wonders for the teacher to share the story of creation? Or, when two boys in the block corner are playing well together, for a teacher to quickly tell them about the friendship of David and Jonathan. Stories told informally, and applied to immediate circumstances, have by far the greatest impact. Then each retelling of the story implants its basic concept more firmly in young alert minds. Teachers need not fear that telling the story several times will lead to boredom. Young children's favorite stories are the ones they know best.

The realistic teacher knows that natural opportunities to share the story will not occur every week in every activity area. Therefore, it is necessary to have a time when everyone hears the Bible story. This will be of value, both to those children who may be hearing it for the first time, and those for whom it is reinforcement of an earlier experience. This is done as the last time block of the session.

When you have more than eight or ten children, it is helpful to divide the class into two or more Bible story groups that meet with a teacher in different parts of the room. These are permanently assigned groups of no more than five to seven children. This arrangement allows children to identify closely with one particular teacher. Children need this sense of added security. With the story being told in these small groups there is ample opportunity for personal interaction between teacher and children.

These Bible story groups sit around a table or form a small circle on the floor. Each teacher presents the Bible story to his or her group, then leads the group in completing the activity page.

Sometimes departments find it necessary to present the Bible story to children in a large group. A shortage of teachers or an overcrowded room are reasons for doing this. The Department Leader may sometimes want to tell the story to the large group while new teachers are becoming accustomed to the children.

If your department has one large story group, you should still divide into small class groups with individual teachers after the Bible story is told. Teachers are then able to talk about the story while leading the groups in completing their activity pages which are provided with the curriculum. (Some groups save the activity page for the second hour, when they use it as one of the activity centers. Children who leave after Sunday School are given the materials to complete at home.)

Step 4—Song and Fun Time

Following completion of the activity page, Song and Fun Time provides a smooth transition to the second hour (Churchtime) program or until parents arrive. The leader or a teacher guides children in activity songs, finger fun, exercises and simple games, as teachers welcome new arrivals or assist those who leave.

SUNDAY SCHOOL FOR 2s THROUGH 5s

Bible Learning Activity Time	Together Time	Bible Story
(Children choose from among small group and individual activities)	(Full department together for music, sharing and special features)	(Each teacher leads small group in Bible Story and activity page)
2s & 3s 40-45 min.	10-15 min.	10-15 min.
4s & 5s 40-45 min.	10-15 min.	15-20 min.
Each time sequence includes the time necessary for moving from one part of the schedule to the next.		

During Song and Fun Time, the children can either remain in their small Bible story groups or gather in one large group for the transition activities until the Churchtime staff is in place. These activities can include coloring, pegs and pegboards, working with dough, stringing beads, working puzzles, listening to music, playing the Autoharp—or even having snacks. With either plan—small groups or large groups—the Sunday School staff remains involved with the children until the Churchtime staff is ready to begin.

The time you have available for Sunday School must be properly utilized for best results. A plan that allows ample time for all parts of the program, and that is operated without rigidity, will insure that the best learning does take place.

Dividing the schedule into three segments gives a good change of pace to keep children from becoming restless. The length of time spent in each segment will vary according to the age level of the children. Four- and five-year-olds are able to spend more time listening than are twos and threes.

CHURCHTIME/THE SECOND HOUR

Sunday School is just one half of most young children's morning at church. The second hour (or Churchtime) is a continuation of the Sunday School's activities through the time of the church worship service. It is a vital part of the Sunday School's ministry to young children, many of whom will remain while their parents attend church. By conducting a second hour, a department doubles the time it has to communicate the teaching/learning objective for that morning. It also enables the department to communicate God's love to children whose parents come only for the worship service.

Instead of sitting through an adult service, or a children's program designed as a "children's church service," or simply being cared for in a baby-sitting program, young children benefit most from interesting learning experiences that reinforce the learning objectives taught in Sunday School. The child feels secure when the Churchtime program is an extension of the Sunday School because there are no abrupt changes in procedure.

What Should Be Done During Churchtime?

Young children need the reinforcement of what they learned in Sunday School more than they need a completely new topic in Churchtime. Sunday morning for the young child should be planned as a continuous, supportive series of learning experiences all pointing towards the same Bible Aims. Churchtime teachers should be aware of the teaching/learning objectives of the Sunday School so they can continue teaching in the same vein, thereby unifying the total morning experience of the child. The Churchtime leader should confer regularly with the Sunday School leader to insure continuity of effort, reinforcing the learning experiences of the earlier session. The basic schedule follows a pattern similar to Sunday School.

CHURCHTIME FOR 2s THROUGH 5s

Song-N-Fun Time	Bible Learning Activity Time	Surprise Time	Wrap-Up Time
Children enjoy a large group time of active songs and games and a snack between Sunday School and Churchtime. 15-20 min.	Following the transition from Sunday School, children choose from Bible Learning Activities. 15-20 min.	Retelling of Bible Story, informal worship experiences, life-related child experience story. 10-15 min.	Large or small group time of activities and games. 5-15 min.

The second hour should include time for Bible Learning Activities, Bible story review, snack, life-related story and large group activity. Bible Learning Activities should take up the largest block of time. As in Sunday School, these activities relate the Bible teaching/learning aims to the child's life.

Song-N-Fun Time ■ Children should remain in the same room they were in for Sunday School, with the same lesson aims. Moving them to a new room can be upsetting to some children.

Since there is often the same number of children, and may even be more during the second hour, it is not a good practice to combine children from several departments during this session. Even if the group is very small, children will benefit more from close, personal attention in a room equipped for their age level.

Children and teachers will be enjoying Song-N-Fun Time in a large group. The Department Leader or a teacher is at the door to welcome new arrivals and to oversee the departure of those who are leaving. The door is kept closed to prevent children from leaving without an adult. Parents should wait outside the room while the leader brings their child to the door.

Each Churchtime teacher arrives as soon as possible after Sunday School and goes directly to the Sunday School teacher he or she is to replace. The Churchtime teacher joins in and then takes over whatever activity is in progress. Teachers who are leaving do so as quickly as possible in order to keep disturbance to a minimum.

At the conclusion of Song-N-Fun Time activities, children may be guided back to the tables for a nutritious snack, and if desired, a brief time of quiet resting. You can avoid disruptive scrambles as the children move from a large group activity to activity areas by using interesting ways of moving only part of the group at once. For example, "Everyone who is wearing black shoes may stand up. Now, each of you with black shoes may find an activity you would like to do. Those with white shoes . . . "

Snack: A light, healthy snack of juice and crackers, cheese slices or fresh fruit or vegetables provides a relaxed time for conversation between teacher and children. (See "Recipes" section for more snack ideas.) This quiet time allows the teacher to become better acquainted with the children by sitting with a small group and enjoying the snack. Children help pass napkins, share apple slices and take turns. A prayer of thanks is always a part of snack time and is most effective when done in small groups. Provision should be made for washing hands before eating. Each child is responsible for disposing of his or her napkin and cup.

Rest: A brief quiet, relaxing time may be of value during the second hour in Early Childhood departments. A few moments of quiet are essential to the well-being of active youngsters. The teachers should sit next to the most restless children to help them by example. A gentle touch and soft words encourage them to rest quietly. If your floor is not carpeted, mats or large towels should be provided. Darken the room slightly and play a recording of soft music. Five to ten minutes is usually ample time, but this can vary depending upon the children's need. Usually the most active children will need these moments most of all. Frantic activity is often a symptom of overstimulation or fatigue. Expect Kindergarten-age children—and those who just arrived at the start of Churchtime—to resist the idea of a rest time. If your group does not seem to want or need a rest, consider a brief time of quiet listening to music later, as part of Surprise Time.

Sometime near the beginning of the session all children should be given the chance to use the toilet. If you do not have a restroom immediately adjacent to your department, time should be set aside for each child to take care of toileting details. Two or three children can be taken together once the crowds are out of the hallways. Even with a restroom that adjoins your department, children may need to be reminded to use the toilet so they will not need to interrupt a group activity later on.

Bible Learning Activity Time ■ As children finish their snack or rest, guide them to choose from two or more activities prepared to continue learning of the same Bible aims as in the first hour. The basic pattern of allowing children to move from one activity to another is followed during the first part of Churchtime just as it was during Sunday School. Again, the number of activities is based on the number of teachers, each one responsible for one area. A department with three or more teachers may repeat one or two activities from the first hour. A small department should have new activities. For example, books could replace puzzles, and blocks could replace Home Living. At least one activity area should always be new for the second hour to keep the children interested.

You may set up one center where a teacher has the Bible story visuals and involves children in retelling the Bible story. Any children who missed the first hour are guided to this center sometime during the session. Some departments also use the children's activity page as a choice at this time if it was not done during the first hour. Be constantly alert for opportunities to weave lesson-related conversation into each activity.

If your church has a patio or outdoor play area, plan some activities for outdoors. Ten to fifteen minutes of muscle-stretching will do wonders for a small child's disposition. On a nice day a walk in the sunshine can be an enjoyable change of pace as well as a valuable learning experience. For example, children may collect nature items to make a collage. If weather or facilities do not allow going outside, another room in the building might be made available for some large muscle play.

Surprise Time ■ When activity materials are put away children and teachers come together for singing and for Bible story review. By this time, children who have been present all morning should know the story well, be familiar with the aim-related songs and understand the main point that is being emphasized.

Provide informal worship experiences at the children's level of understanding. Include songs which deal clearly with the Bible aims, conversation about the Bible verse, games or movement activities and a review of the Bible story. Let the children know that you are aware they have heard the story before. Your enthusiasm and interest in the story will keep even the most sophisticated kindergartener from being bored. You may want to involve children in helping you tell parts of the story, act it out or move visual aids to illustrate the story. See Chapter 12, "Effective Storytelling," for tips on story presentations.

A life-related story may also be told at this time. This story should relate the Bible teaching/learning aims of the morning in life experiences familiar to the child. Songs and finger fun used earlier can also be repeated here.

Wrap-Up Time ■ To conclude the morning, children may remain in the large group for activity songs, games and exercises. The same activities used between Sunday School and Churchtime can be repeated. Or, you may use simple activities that can be cleaned up quickly, so that each child can easily put away materials when his or her parents arrive. The leader or a teacher should be at the door and bring each child to meet parents outside the room.

Whether children are in large or small groups, it is important for them to stay involved until their parents come for them. Occasionally an insecure or exhausted child may begin to cry when parents come for other children. Reassure this child that Mom or Dad will be coming soon. Try to involve the child in an activity such as rocking a doll or looking at a picture book. Remain with the child until parents do arrive. A toddler or two-year-old may need the security of being held on your lap.

Give each child a warm, personal good-bye. Be sure to use the child's name. Have a pleasant, positive comment for parents also. If parents wish to visit, ask them to wait until all the children have left or make an appointment to talk with them during the week.

After the children leave, take a few minutes to be sure materials are put away and everything is in order. While you straighten things up, talk with other teachers about the session and exchange suggestions to improve next week.

SUNDAY NIGHTS

If your church wants young parents to attend an evening service, provision should be made for young children. Most children this age, at the end of a busy day, are even less capable of sitting through an adult service than they are in the morning. Establishing and maintaining a Sunday evening program for young children requires additional effort, but if your church is committed to reaching young families the results are well worth the work.

First, secure adequate personnel. Three basic plans are in common use:

1. Develop an evening staff that functions on a regular basis in the same way as the Sunday School teachers.

2. Use a variation of the morning second hour program by having volunteers serve for a month at a time.

3. Operate with paid personnel. Paid personnel usually provide child care only. Other arrangements would have to be made to provide learning experiences for the children.

The location for your Sunday night program should be the same as for Sunday morning. Since there will probably be a smaller number of young children in the evening, it may be best to combine two or more age groups. Keep in mind that it is better to have two small groups, each of similar age, than one large group with a wider range.

When the same rooms are used in the evening as in the morning, there must be coordination between the two programs as to the use of facilities and equipment. Foster a cooperative spirit of sharing based on mutual respect for both programs. All groups should observe the same careful treatment of materials and equipment. A periodic meeting of the leaders of both programs is a valuable means of coordinating.

The same Bible story and learning goals can be used in both evening and morning programs. Young children thrive on the familiar. The opportunity to repeat an enjoyable experience will be eagerly anticipated. If two groups of different ages have been combined, use the material designed for the younger group. Teacher's Manuals should be given to all teachers.

Activities on Sunday evening are basically the same as for the morning programs. One new activity should be added to spark interest. Planning this requires communication with Sunday School leaders.

A sample schedule for threes through fives, based on a 75-minute program, would be:

Small Group Activities	45 minutes
Snack and Rest	15 minutes
Large Group Time	15 minutes

These time blocks would vary with the length of the service and the age of the children. Children under three do not need a large group time.

THE MIDWEEK PROGRAM

A weeknight program for birth through three years should follow the pattern for Sunday nights.

Fours and fives in many churches are provided with a choir or club program during this time. As a cooperative effort of the music department and education department, the objective of an Early Childhood Choir is to develop musical skills and appreciation, not to produce a performing group. Time should be spent in the regular activity areas, with music being interwoven into these learning experiences. The concepts of the songs to be sung that evening are part of the teachers' conversations in each area. Special emphasis is given to art activities related to the songs.

The large group time emphasis is on music experiences. Listening to records and various instruments, singing, humming, marching and experimenting with simple instruments should be included. Rhythm instruments are good sources of meaningful firsthand music experiences.

There must always be communication and coordination among all Early Childhood program leaders. Whenever a child comes to church he or she should be greeted with friendly, loving care. Also, the same behavior should be expected of the child. Consistent standards in all Early Childhood departments build a sense of security and confidence in young children.

PART 3

Skills and Tips for Better Teaching

Active Learning for Active Children

A young boy was asked by his mother what he had learned in Sunday School. "Nothing," was his reply.

"Nothing?" his mother asked. "Didn't Miss Bowers teach you *something*?"

"She tried," the boy admitted. "She made us sit, and she taught us and taught us and taught us and I got so tired I couldn't learn *anything*!"

Young children are not very efficient at learning while quietly sitting and listening. They are highly skilled at learning through firsthand activity. This chapter describes each of the Bible Learning Activities which provide the child's "doing" during the session. These activities involve the child in familiar experiences from home and preschool. Touching, smelling, building, pretending and gluing are just a few of the ways the child plays. He or she can then be guided by an alert teacher who is ready to connect the child's play to the session's Bible aims.

Bible Learning Activities help the child:

- feel comfortable with familiar materials and activities which meet the God-given needs to move and explore;
- interact positively with other children and teachers, building relationships which help the child understand the biblical concepts of love, kindness, sharing and giving;
- connect new Bible truths to familiar experiences;
- apply Bible truths in practical situations;
- remember information, because it has been presented in a setting that is meaningful to the child;
- talk easily about God, Jesus, the Bible and prayer in the

midst of normal activity (see Deut. 6:6,7);
- experience success at his or her own level, building healthy attitudes and expectations;
- enjoy learning at church, creating a desire to come again and again.

TIPS FOR ALL BIBLE LEARNING ACTIVITIES

1. Up through five children can comfortably work at one time on a Bible Learning Activity. Limiting the number of children that can participate in an activity at one time helps foster good social relationships and allows the teacher to give individual guidance to this small group. This can be accomplished in several ways.
- Provide only the number of chairs for the size group the activity can allow.
- Post at the child's eye level a sign with the numeral 4. The teacher can assist children as they count out four participants.
- Use masking tape or sheets of paper to define work areas on a table.

2. The number of Bible Learning Activities offered during a session depends on the needs of the children as well as the size of the class. In Sunday School and Churchtime, a class of 15 to 20 children should be offered four to six Bible Learning Activities throughout the course of the entire morning. A smaller class of six or eight children would need at least two choices, with perhaps a third one for variety and interest.

3. It is important that each Bible Learning Activity is guided by a teacher. Activity assignments may be made on a unit basis. For example: One teacher will plan and carry out a Home Living Bible Learning Activity for four weeks (or one unit of lessons). As each Bible Learning Activity is led by a teacher, children move freely from one area of the room to another, participating in or completing several activities during the session. Teachers are

not just "watching" or "caring for" children while they "play," but rather acting as facilitators of the learning that is taking place during this valuable block of time. The teacher's role in Bible Learning Activities is to use conversation about the child's actions to guide the child's thoughts toward specific Bible aims.

Guiding Conversation During Activities

Guiding conversation is the key ingredient in making Bible Learning Activities effective teaching tools. The teacher's role in every activity is to use comments and questions designed to engage the child in dialogue about what the child is doing and about the Bible aims. Combining words with actions in a relaxed climate greatly increases a child's ability to respond to Bible truth. Through guided conversation you not only increase a child's knowledge and understanding, but also help the child build positive attitudes about self, about others and about church.

In communicating with children, you convey ideas through your actions as well as your words. In fact nonverbal messages are more powerful, many times, than verbal messages. As you seek to create a learning environment where children are guided in experiences toward spiritual truths, there are a number of communication skills which will help you to be successful in your efforts.

1. Use a natural tone of voice. Don't talk down to children. Avoid sugary sweet words.

2. Give direct eye contact when speaking to a child. Kneel, bend or sit if necessary to focus on the child.

3. Use the child's name often.

4. Touching and smiling are very important.

5. Actively listen to what a child is saying. You can accomplish this by repeating or rephrasing the child's words, or by asking a question about what the child said to encourage further conversation.

6. Keep your Bible-related aim in mind as you talk to children about what they are doing.

- Encourage children to talk about what they are doing and thinking.
- Ask questions which stimulate children to think about the Bible verse or Bible story.
- Comment on ways the child's actions demonstrate the Bible verse or a part of the Bible story.
- Look for opportunities to tell the Bible story while children work.
- As children work, sing a song which expresses the Bible aim.

7. Use your example, or model, to create understanding. Children will do what they see you doing. An example combined with an explanation is strikingly effective in influencing both understanding and attitudes.

8. Accept a child's feelings and ideas.

- Support and encourage the process rather than the product.
- Affirm a child's happy feelings and recognize negative feelings during an activity. ("You really don't like working with finger paint, do you? You might want to play with the blocks, or read a book.")
- Value children's work and effort whether or not the work is done correctly or completed to perfection.
- Be careful about correcting a child's mistake or wrong answer. Either find some element that is correct to affirm, or ask questions that will help the child think through what was done or said.

9. Use praise and encouragement to motivate a child toward success. Positive comments about specific efforts and actions encourage children to want to do the right thing. Focusing on a child's strengths and assets builds strong feelings of acceptance and self-worth. Children are naturally eager to please; they thrive on being noticed in positive ways.

10. Help children make choices and decisions. However, don't offer a choice when there really isn't one. "It's time to put your blocks away" is more useful than, "Would you like to put

blocks away now?" Even better is, "It's time to clean up our room. Would you like to put away blocks, or help wash out paintbrushes?"

Keep in mind that guided conversation during a learning activity usually takes practice before it begins to feel natural. If you use these guidelines, your Bible Learning Activities will soon come alive for children as you informally direct children's thoughts to the Bible truth you want them to learn. No longer will learning activities seem like projects, or just play times, but times of valuable and enriching Bible learning.

The following pages present a variety of Bible Learning Activities. The materials needed for each activity plus ways to accomplish specific Bible learning aims through these activities are included. Guidance is given about the age-level appropriateness of each activity.

BLOCK BUILDING

Blocks are important learning tools for toddlers through fives, both boys and girls. Blocks help a child develop physically, mentally, socially and spiritually. Building with blocks allows a child to work alone, parallel with another child or in cooperation with others in a small group. Lifting and carrying blocks helps satisfy the need for large muscle activity. Block building helps a child to develop ideas and to make decisions. A child's imagination allows blocks to become a car, a train, a house or a fire station. The child also learns responsibility in caring for materials.

Block building provides opportunities for cooperation and sharing and learning to respect the rights and ideas of others. Blocks provide opportunities for problem solving and decision making. Block building provides firsthand experiences in practicing Christian concepts, such as sharing, helping, taking turns and exercising self-control. Provide enough blocks so several children can enjoy block building at the same time.

Block building provides the teacher opportunities to relate the lesson's Bible aims to the child's interests and activities. At the block area you can occasionally initiate building projects to help children become familiar with Bible-time life. For instance, on a Sunday when a house will be mentioned in the Bible story, show a picture of a Bible-time house, guide children in building one from blocks and pretending to "walk" people up to the roof. By familiarizing them with the idea of a flat-roofed house, when they hear it mentioned in the story later in the morning, they can listen with understanding.

Expect a *toddler* or *two-year-old* to hold a block or carry one around the room. The child enjoys holding one in each hand and banging them together and piling one block on top of another and knocking them down. A two-year-old may use blocks as steps or place them end to end and walk on them.

A *three-year-old* often uses several blocks at a time, stacking them merely for the pleasure of stacking and sometimes attaching a name to what is being built. The pile of blocks becomes whatever the child names it, changing its identity from moment to moment.

The *four-year-old* and *five-year-old* child is beginning to plan what to build and how to build it. Imagination becomes involved in playing out an event with the construction. The child enjoys using accessory toys such as boats and trucks along with block building. The five-year-old is able to construct a building with walls, doors, windows and a roof. The child can be encouraged to build more realistically through suggestions such as, "What do you need in your building so the people can get inside?"

Materials ■ **Blocks:** Toddlers enjoy using large, soft fabric blocks. Both toddlers and twos work well with large, hollow cardboard blocks. Blocks for children under three should be lightweight and easy to manipulate. Suitable blocks can be made from empty milk cartons and cardboard boxes. Tightly stuff these cartons and boxes with wadded newspapers, then cover them with adhesive-backed paper. Threes are interested in building more complex projects; they need blocks of various shapes and sizes. A set of unit blocks, in which all block sizes are based on related measurements (two blocks of one size equal one block of the next size, etc., as in sketch) is a versatile learning tool that stimulates creative building. Since four- and five-year-old children build quite ambitious structures, they need a larger number and variety of blocks.

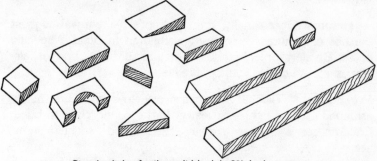

Standard size for the unit block is 2¾-inch square,
1⅜-inch thickness (6.9 × 3.45 cm).

Wooden blocks are durable and may be purchased in sets or made from scrap lumber. Carefully sand each piece. When wooden blocks show signs of wear they can be sanded and refinished. They will last many years and are worth the investment.

Accessory toys: Toddlers and twos tend to use each toy—a block or a truck—independent of other toys. However, these children will enjoy using toys in the same area with the blocks. The value of block building is enhanced for the threes, fours and fives by a variety of accessory toys which encourage dramatic play.

Sturdy transportation toys should be a part of every block area. Wooden cars and trucks are preferable to most metal ones for safety and durability.

Other accessory toys include furniture and stand-up figures of people, animals and trees. These items can be purchased or made by gluing appropriate magazine pictures to pieces of wood or cardboard. Pieces of thin plywood or corrugated cardboard,

12 × 12 inches (30 × 30 cm), encourage the building of ramps, roofs, etc.

Fives and some fours enjoy using signs ("Airport," "Gas Station," "Church," etc.) in dramatic play. Keep a felt pen and large index cards handy to make new signs. Signs should be printed in upper and lower case lettering.

Pictures: Occasionally, your Teacher's Manual will suggest the use of pictures to encourage children to build a specific object. Be alert for large, colorful pictures of boats, bridges, airplanes, etc., to add to your picture file.

Procedure ■ Blocks and accessory toys that are neatly arranged on low, open shelves invite the young child to build. Children can easily see what is available and can help themselves to the desired pieces.

The floor in the block area should be carpeted with a smooth rug to provide a warm, level surface for building while at the same time reducing noise from falling blocks.

The child should be free to choose what to build, setting the stage for relating his or her interest to the day's Bible learning aims. A teacher is nearby to offer guidance when needed.

Putting away blocks and accessory toys usually takes more time than other cleanup activities. Warn the children in advance that it's almost cleanup time. Guide children in stacking like-sized blocks together. Pieces of woodgrained adhesive-backed paper, cut the shape of the blocks and attached to shelves, will mark the place where each size block should be stored.

Bible Teaching/Learning Opportunities ■ How can the teacher use block building to relate Bible aims to a child's activity? Here are several conversation examples to fit typical lesson emphases:

Kindness/Sharing: As children work with blocks, comment on specific acts of sharing and kindness. "Maria and Shannon, you girls are having such a good time playing together. You are sharing the blocks with each other. Our Bible says to share what we have with others." When introducing the Bible story later, remind children of specific acts you observed. "This morning I saw Eric do a kind thing for Kim. Eric moved over to give Kim room to build with blocks. I'm glad Eric was kind and I'm glad I know a Bible story about a man who was kind."

Bible verses for your conversation:
"Be . . . ready to share" (1 Tim. 6:18 *NASB*).
"Love each other" (John 15:12).
"Be kind . . . to one another" (Eph. 4:32).

Church: As several children worked with blocks, Mr. Cassidy began to sing, "Church time, church time, time to come to church." Rebecca looked up and smiled. "Rebecca, you look happy to be working and playing at church. Let's tell God we like to work at church." Rebecca and Mr. Cassidy bowed their heads. After they had both said, "Dear God, I like to work at church," Rebecca went happily back to her play.

Bible verses for your conversation:
Jesus said, "Come . . . and learn from me" (Matt. 11:28,29).
"Come, let us worship the Lord" (Ps. 95:6 *NASB*).
"We love Jesus." (See John 4:19.)

GOD'S WONDERS

Young children are bursting with curiosity! "Let me see!" (touch, taste, hear, smell) is their familiar plea. Discovery is an integral part of the young child's life. Exploring God's wonders helps a child begin to sense the extent of God's love, care and wisdom.

The wonder and excitement of nature presents a variety of opportunities to help the young child learn about God and self. When a child looks at seeds growing or a butterfly struggling out of its cocoon, simply say, "All things were made by God" (see John 1:3). After seeing the beauty in the design of a single snow-flake, lead the child to respond naturally by saying, "Thank you, God, for making snowflakes." Your conversations help the child learn to associate God with these experiences.

The presence of nature materials can help an insecure child feel more comfortable in a new situation. If there is a live animal at the display, the child often focuses on the animal and forgets about feeling alone. *Babies* enjoy looking at and touching a flower or a leaf. A goldfish's movements may fascinate a child. Introduce babies to living items one at time—always kept in the teacher's hand.

The *toddler* or *two-year-old* will approach the God's Wonders display in a very simple way. At first the child may pick up an object, look at it from all angles and maybe try to taste it. (Avoid pebbles, seeds and other things which may be small enough to swallow and supervise carefully when plant leaves may be tasted!) Then the child may put the object down and move on to another activity. Expect children to return to the table several times during the morning and repeat the procedure.

The *three-year-old* continues to explore the wonders of God's world with increased interest, showing curiosity and asking questions.

Most *fours and fives* can participate in activities repeated over several weeks. These activities might include growing plants from seeds or watching a caterpillar change into a butterfly.

Materials and Procedures ■ Materials can be effectively displayed on a low shelf or table, near a window if possible. Growing plants or a simple aquarium are ever-changing sources of wonder. Living animals and birds, seasonal surprises such as autumn leaves and seeds, a pan of snow, icicles, shells and flowers offer a child a firsthand experience in investigating God's wonders. A good quality magnifying glass, a magnet and colorful pictures of nature scenes are worthwhile additions to your God's Wonders display.

Have simple books about rocks, shells, animals, birds, reptiles, etc., clearly and accurately illustrated for a readily available source of information as you guide children in discovering God's wonders.

Nature walks: Use a walking rope to keep children together. (A walking rope is a length of rope with knots tied 2 feet [60 cm] apart. The children hold onto it as they walk. Explain clearly and simply its purpose so children know what they are expected to do.) Bring containers for any specimen you find along the way. To make your walk a valuable learning experience, suggest something specific for which the children can look. Remind children to choose things already on the ground—not leaves, flowers and grasses that are still growing.

As you walk along, talk about the things you see. Avoid hurrying the children. Stop for a closer look at flowers, an insect or a rock. Relate what the children see to the orderliness of God's world, His care for the things He has made. "God planned for many trees to lose their leaves in the fall. In the spring the trees will grow new leaves."

Planting: Indoor gardens can be grown from parts of *fruits and vegetables.* Save the top inch of carrots, beets, turnips or rutabagas. Stand the tips in a shallow dish of water. Use small pebbles to support the plant. Within a few days small white roots will appear and fern-like leaves will begin to grow. *Seeds* that will grow quickly are grass, lettuce, radish, lima bean, lentil, nasturtium, pumpkin, melon and marigolds.

Use unbreakable, wide-bottom containers for planters. You will also need a supply of planter mix or soil, newspapers and watering cans. An important accessory in a planting experience is a magnifying glass.

Place a *sweet potato,* pointed end down, in a jar of water. Use a transparent plastic or glass container so roots will be visible. Leave about one-third of the potato above water. Insert several toothpicks if necessary to keep the potato from sinking. The potato will root and in about 10 days vines will begin to grow. *Avocado* seeds and *onions* can be planted in a similar way. Avocados may take up to 3 months to sprout—be patient! They grow into beautiful plants.

Some seeds can be planted so the children can see them germinate. Roll a piece of paper towel and put it inside a glass. The paper should touch the sides of the glass. Then fill the center of the glass with damp sand. Slip several *lima beans* between the paper and the glass (see sketch). Keep the sand moist. The children will have a clear view of the roots and root hairs. Beans may also be "planted" in egg cartons between pieces of soaking wet cotton. Allow a few days for them to sprout.

For a *hanging garden,* cut an orange in half and scoop out the inside. With an ice pick, poke three holes near the rim to string yarn through for a hanger. Let the children spoon potting soil into the orange halves, then sprinkle grass seed on top or plant three sprouting lima beans.

Magnets: Have a horseshoe magnet and two bar magnets available for four- and five-year-old children to use for *experiments.*

Provide a variety of objects, some of which will adhere to the magnet and some that will not. Also have two boxes, one marked yes and one marked no. Place a variety of objects in a shallow box or on the table. The child can experiment to see what the magnet will or will not attract. Objects the magnet attracts are placed in the box marked yes. "Did the paper clip stick to the magnet? God planned for things made of iron or steel to stick to magnets."

For further experiments provide a piece of heavy paper, a glass or jar of water, a small pane of glass (bind the edges of the glass with masking tape to prevent cut fingers), a handkerchief, a dish of sand or dirt and paper clips. Ask, "Will this paper clip stick to the magnet through a piece of paper? Let's find out." Lay a piece of paper over a paper clip. Use the magnet to lift the paper clip and paper. Repeat the experiment using the pane of glass. After that experiment, try these. Lay the paper clip on top of the paper or pane of glass. Let a child hold the magnet underneath. As the child moves the magnet the paper clip will move. Let a child pick up a paper clip or other iron object with a magnet wrapped in a handkerchief or use a magnet to retrieve a paper clip from a glass of water.

Children enjoy playing *games involving magnets.* For "Find the Nail" provide drinking straws, three or four large finishing nails and toothpicks. Place a nail in each of three or four straws. Place toothpicks in the remaining straws. Staple the ends of the straws to keep the nails and toothpicks from falling out. Place the straws in a box. The children take turns using the magnet to find the straws containing nails.

Water: Water play is an ideal outdoor activity. With proper protection of the floor and tabletops, water play can be a successful indoor activity as well. A large sheet of plastic will protect floors and carpets; plastic tableclothes will protect tabletops.

An apron, a small container (such as a sandpail) of water and a wide brush are all the equipment needed for the young child to experiment with *water painting.* Let the child paint outside walls, sidewalks, outdoor equipment or large sheets of masonite.

Toddlers and two-year-olds enjoy "catching" soap bubbles. Children three and up enjoy *blowing bubbles.* To prepare your own inexpensive bubble solution, mix water with liquid detergent in paper cups. Give each child a cup of soapy water and a drinking straw. Demonstrate blowing air through the straw. Keep a sponge handy to wipe up spills. The children will also enjoy mixing the soapy water with a rotary beater. A few drops of food coloring will make colorful bubbles.

Moving their hands through water and slowly *pouring water* from one container to another seems to have a calming effect on most young children. They enjoy the feel and the fun of water. Provide a large plastic tub or basin of water and plastic eyedroppers, funnels, unbreakable measuring cups, squeeze bottles and soup ladles. The children will experiment with pouring, measuring, squirting and washing. Some will be content to just wiggle their fingers in the cool water. (Bathing dolls, washing dishes and scrubbing tabletops is an excellent enrichment activity for the Home Living center.) "How does the water feel, Megan? I'm glad God made the cool water. Does this cup hold as much water as that cup, Eric? Which cup holds the most water? You're using the eyes God gave you to see how much water is in each cup."

For an experiment involving *frozen water,* give each child a paper cup containing one or two ice cubes. Talk about how the ice feels (cold, hard, wet, slippery) and of what the ice is made. "Who made the water? All things were made by God! What is ice? Ice is water that has been frozen solid. Why do we need ice? What happens when ice is left out of the freezer?" Place the cups outside in the sunshine. At the end of the hour check to see what has happened to the ice.

Children enjoy *experimenting* with all kinds of objects to determine which objects float and which ones sink. Let the children take turns placing objects (some that float, some that sink—rock, cork, marble, sponge, twig, spoon, etc.) in a large container of water. Before each child puts an object in the water, ask, "Will the (feather) sink or float?" Objects sink when they are heavy enough to push aside the water in which they are placed. It is sufficient at this time to simply state, "God made some objects to float and some to sink." Give brief, meaningful facts rather than a long, dull explanation.

Senses: For activities involving the sense of *touch*, provide babies and toddlers with blocks, balls or pillows covered with a variety of fabrics: satin, terry cloth, wool, fur, etc. Older children enjoy a "feel walk," in which they take off their shoes and walk over a variety of textured materials and describe how each feels. Fours and fives may do the walk blindfolded.

Threes through fives enjoy reaching into a bag or box and identifying familiar objects only by feel. Twos and younger threes can do this if they see the objects before they are put in the bag. "You guessed what that was just by using your fingers. I'm glad God made our fingers so we can feel with them."

For activities involving *sight,* provide baby food jars half full of water. Guide the children in adding food coloring with water droppers to make the color desired. It usually takes three drops for dark colors and more for yellow. Next try mixing colors. "Watch what happens when you squeeze a little blue into the yellow . . . . What color is it now? God made our eyes to see beautiful colors."

Play a color guessing game. Teacher sings (to the tune of "Here We Go Round the Mulberry Bush"):

"Look around the room with me
The room with me, the room with me.
Look around the room with me.
I see something (red)."

The children take turns guessing various objects. The one who guesses correctly picks an object and whispers it in the teacher's ear. She sings the song, putting in the child's name: "Look around the room with (Kim), she sees something (blue)."

For activities involving *hearing,* use a cassette recorder to tape common household sounds: doorbell, phone, vacuum cleaner, pots and pans, etc. Play a sound for the children to identify. Give clues and replay sounds when necessary. Bring a tape recorder and tape the children singing or individuals talking; then play it back for them to hear. "Rachel, I can hear your voice singing on the tape recorder. God gave us ears to hear."

Talk about various things children use their ears for at home and at church. "I like to listen to singing at church. It makes me happy to hear glad songs about Jesus."

Play a listening game for threes. Give one simple direction at a time: stand on one leg, put your hand on your head, touch your nose. Commend children for listening and following instructions.

For activities involving the sense of *smell,* make "I Can Smell" booklets. Saturate pieces of felt with aromas, such as peppermint, clove, lemon, perfume, etc. The child glues the felt inside a folded sheet of paper to make a booklet. Children smell each other's booklets to identify odors.

For activities involving *taste,* provide bite-sized pieces of fruit and vegetables. With fours and fives, blindfold one child at a time, giving one thing to taste and identify. Ask children, "Is it sweet or sour? Is it warm or cold?"

Animal life: There is a wide variety of animal life that can be brought into the classroom. In the summer you can make an *earthworm farm.* Put a quart jar inside a gallon jar. Fill the smaller jar with sand to weight it down. Fill the space between both jars with loose, damp soil and five or six large worms. Put black paper around the outside of the larger jar for a week. In the darkness the worms behave as if they are underground. When you take the paper off the next Sunday, you will be able to observe tunnels the worms have made. Keep the dirt moist by adding a little water each week.

Insects, such as caterpillars, can be kept in large jars with air holes in the lid. Leaves from the tree on which they were found should be included. Food needs vary. Ladybugs eat aphids. Crickets eat bread crumbs, raisins and lettuce. Grasshoppers thrive on leaves, bread crumbs and even orange peels. All insects need water.

Fish are easy to care for in a bowl or aquarium. Provide commercially-packaged fish food. **Birds** such as parakeets or canaries are also excellent visitors to Sunday School departments.

Place the insect, animal or bird in an area where the children can view it easily. As the children watch, call their attention to specific things about the insect or animal. "See how the toad flicks out his tongue to catch his food. God made the toad's tongue in a very special way." "The caterpillar is beginning to spin his cocoon. He is spinning the thread round and round his body just as God planned." Children can share in the care of animal life by helping clean cages, bringing food and feeding the animal with the teacher's guidance. After a few Sundays of observance, the insects and animals should be returned to their natural habitats.

Bible Teaching/Learning Opportunities ■ The child's natural interest and curiosity in God's wonders provides endless opportunities for you to share what God's Word says and how it relates to the child's life. These examples show ways to relate God's Wonders activities to a variety of Bible topics:

Creation: All God's Wonders activities are easily related to lessons on creation. It is God who made the hands to feel, the ears to hear, etc. Magnetism, the refraction of light in a prism and the ability of water to support weight are all part of God's creation.

"What are you using to smell the lemon, Jason? God made our noses so we can smell lemons and flowers and all kinds of things. All things were made by God . . . . What do the plants need to grow? God made the sun and rain to help the plants grow."

Bible verses for your conversation:
"He has made everything beautiful" (Eccles. 3:11).
"The Lord has done great things for us; we are glad" (Ps. 126:3, *NASB*).
"He gives rain on the earth" (Job 5:10, *NASB*).

Thankfulness: Young children respond naturally to the wonder and awe of God's creation. This response of mind and heart easily becomes one of thankfulness. "How does the rain help us? God gives rain on the earth. We can tell God thank you for the rain . . . . I thank God for our eyes. Tell us one thing you can see with the eyes God gave you . . . . This cool water feels good on a hot day like today. We can tell God thank you for the water. Our Bible tells us it is good to give thanks to the Lord."

Bible verses for your conversation:
"I thank God" (2 Tim. 1:3).
"Give thanks to the Lord, for He is good" (Ps. 136:1).
"It is good to sing praises to our God" (Ps. 147:1, *NASB*).

BOOKS

Provide a quiet area where children can look at books during Bible Learning Activities. Books may also be used to supplement other activities and during Together Time.

Books are important learning tools for all children. They bring pleasure, create ideas, stimulate curiosity and help children solve problems. Books help the young child develop an awareness of words. They provide opportunities for close physical contact between a teacher and child. Happy experiences with colorful, interesting books help create a desire to read.

Children enjoy looking at books alone or hearing the book read by the teacher. Books for young children are most effective when they reinforce firsthand learning experiences. Books about familiar objects and events are best.

Babies and toddlers need books with simple, colorful and realistic pictures. The teacher of babies should make very simple comments about the pictures. With toddlers, ask the child to point to items as you name them.

Twos and threes are still primarily interested in the pictures. The child will often point to one object in a picture and name it. Although younger children are usually anxious to go on to the next page, they enjoy responding to simple questions about the picture. Teachers can help build vocabulary by repeating the child's reply in a complete sentence and sometimes adding a descriptive word. "What is this, Kim? That's right. It's a cat. It's a yellow cat. God made the yellow cat."

Fours and fives enjoy looking at the pictures in a book while hearing a brief story. Select storybooks with no more than a few sentences per page. Many children are aware of the words on the page. A child may ask, "What does this word say?" Five-year-olds are learning to recognize some words and may happily announce, "I know that word! That word is 'stop.'"

Encourage fours and fives to use books for research. "There is a book about insects on our bookshelf. Let's see if it tells about this ladybug."

Materials ■ A good selection of books provides opportunities to widen a child's horizons to relate Scripture truth to areas of interest and experience. Choose books which relate to the focus of a unit of lessons so they can be used over several weeks. Check your curriculum for recommended book lists as your guide in purchasing books for your department. Select picture books with large, clear, colorful pictures and a minimum of detail. Books for babies and toddlers should be of cloth or vinyl to survive being chewed and pulled. These books should be wiped or washed after use each week.

Books for twos and threes should have a few words on each page. Stories should be about familiar subjects, such as animals, babies and families; and about familiar activities, such as playing, helping, eating and sleeping. Books for fours and fives may also include pictures and stories about nature, machines and children from other lands. Simple stories about Jesus can be included for all ages.

The Bible is the most important book in the room. Provide a large Bible in which you have inserted the pictures from the child's curriculum materials. Insert these pictures next to the appropriate Scripture passage. Use a highlighter pen to lightly shade the story. Also mark verses used in conversation.

Children enjoy making their own books, using magazine pictures or their own art. They will often return many times to look at books they helped put together.

Procedure ■ With babies, take a book to the rocking chair, crib or playpen to show the child. With toddlers and older children, display books where children can see and reach them. Limit the number of books you display; too many simply confuse a child. Three to five is a good number for toddlers and twos. Older children may use up to seven or eight. All books used should relate to the current unit of lessons.

Books should be attractively arranged in a quiet area of the room, where a child can browse through a book alone or join two or three others to listen to a story. Unless a teacher is nearby to read the text or talk about the picture, a child has "seen" a book in a few seconds. As you look at a picture book with a child, ask questions that will stimulate observation and thought. "What sound does a dog make? What is the kitten wearing around its neck? Why do you think the girl looks sad?"

A book rack with slanting shelves is ideal for displaying a few books. It also provides space in the back for storing books not in use.

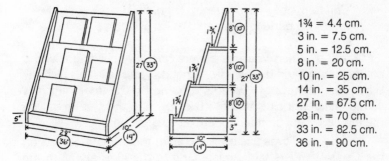

1¾ = 4.4 cm.
3 in. = 7.5 cm.
5 in. = 12.5 cm.
8 in. = 20 cm.
10 in. = 25 cm.
14 in. = 35 cm.
27 in. = 67.5 cm.
28 in. = 70 cm.
33 in. = 82.5 cm.
36 in. = 90 cm.

Circled figures are for 3s through 5s; others for toddlers and 2s.

Place an appropriate book at an interest center and encourage the children to use it for reference. "This book is about many different kinds of rocks. Maybe we can find a picture of our rocks in the book."

Use the picture Bible in the book area. Young children can know that the Bible is a special book that tells us about God and Jesus. They will enjoy looking through the Bible and recognizing pictures that illustrate a favorite story. Bible storybooks with clear, accurate pictures help children know of Bible-time customs, clothing, homes, etc.

Bible Teaching/Learning Opportunities ■ Sharing/Helping:

When your lesson's Bible aims involve sharing, kindness or helping, select books with stories about children who demonstrate these kinds of behavior. In your conversation encourage the child to talk about what is happening in the story or pictures and relate the happenings to Scripture truth. "What is the boy doing? When we rake the leaves we are helping. Our Bible tells us to help each other."

The use of books provides opportunities for children to share, to help and to be kind. "Rosa, you are kind to move over so Kyle can see the book, too. Lisa, thank you for choosing this book. We will enjoy looking at it with you."

Bible verses for your conversation:
"Children, obey your parents" (Eph. 6:1).
"Let us do good to all people" (Gal. 6:10).

Creation: When you use picture books about animals and nature for twos and threes, ask, "What do you see in this picture? Who made the puppy? What is growing on the tree?" (To give young children a clue, point to the object in the picture as you mention it.) "God planned for apples to grow on trees."

As fours and fives use books to learn more about objects on the God's Wonders table, relate God to the illustrations in the book. "Bees carry pollen from flower to flower. God planned for bees to help new plants to grow. The tiny sea animal that lived in this shell built his shell larger and larger as he grew. God planned it that way."

In the picture Bible point out Bible words that relate to creation. "This is the part of the Bible that tells us that God made our beautiful world. Right here it says, 'God made the sky!' See these words? They tell us that all things were made by God."

Bible verses for your conversation:
"God . . . made the world" (Acts 17:24).
"God gives us all things to enjoy." (See 1 Tim. 6:17.)
"Everything God created is good" (1 Tim. 4:4).

PUZZLES

"Look! I did it!" Seth shouts as he completes a puzzle. Puzzles help satisfy a child's desire to achieve. They provide an opportunity for the child to work alone or with one or two friends. Using puzzles helps a child learn to think, to reason and to solve problems. Puzzles help the child learn to work independently and to develop eye-hand coordination. Through using puzzles a child can enjoy a sense of achievement as well as learn to share and take turns. Puzzles also help develop visual discrimination skills, an important aspect of learning to read. Help the children lay out the pieces on the left side of the puzzle to encourage developing left-to-right eye coordination.

Materials ■ *Toddlers* enjoy puzzles such as stacking rings and nesting boxes. Older toddlers and *twos* can succeed with flat puzzles with three or four pieces. Each puzzle piece is a picture of a whole object (a bunny, a ball, etc.). The child will press the piece against the puzzle frame, maneuvering it until it falls into place. *Threes, fours and fives* can work puzzles with pieces that are parts of a whole object. The complexity of the puzzle used depends upon the child's patience, coordination and dexterity, not necessarily his or her age. *Wooden inlay puzzles* are the best jigsaw puzzles because of their durability and ease of use. Most puzzles for two-year-old children should have a maximum of 4-6 pieces; threes, 6-12 pieces; fours, 10-15 pieces; fives, 10-plus pieces. Each department should offer puzzles of varying degrees of difficulty to allow for the varying abilities of the children.

Puzzles should be colorful with simple, realistic pictures. Select puzzles that depict places and things familiar to children. A puzzle rack is a worthwhile investment. It helps keep puzzle pieces from becoming lost; children learn quickly to take only one puzzle from the rack at a time and to put it back when they have finished.

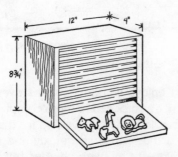

4 in. = 10 cm.
8¾ in. = 22.1 cm.
12 in. = 30 cm.

If a piece is lost, make a replacement from plastic wood. Press aluminum foil into the place where the piece fits. Fill the foil with the plastic wood. When it dries, sand off any rough edges, then paint the piece.

Felt boards are an interesting puzzle variation. Cover a 10×12-inch (25×30-cm) piece of plywood with solid-colored felt. Cut objects such as geometric shapes, houses, churches, trains, trees, flowers, birds, butterflies, cats, dogs, boys, girls, etc., out of different types of materials (wallpaper samples, satin, leather, sandpaper, velvet, fur). Back them with felt. Children may make their own pictures with the figures. Encourage them to tell stories about their creations. Or you may play a matching game. The teacher or a child chooses a figure and places it on the board. The others find one with the same texture or color and put it in the same place on another board.

A unique kind of puzzle that captures the interest of young children is a *gadget board*. To make a gadget board, sand and varnish a 12×48×1-inch (30×120×2.5-cm) board. Attach (with screws) hardware items commonly used about the house, such as door hook, slide lock, light switch, etc. Place gadget board on low table so several children at a time can use it.

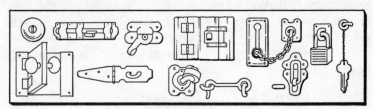

Also provide manipulative toys (e.g., Legos, etc.), peg boards and large beads for stringing.

Procedure ■ A child enjoys working puzzles over and over again, gaining confidence to proceed to more complicated ones. Have a more difficult puzzle ready and waiting for that moment. "Adam, you completed that puzzle so quickly and so easily! I have a new puzzle for you. It's a little bit harder, but I know you can do it." Remain nearby to give encouragement. Praise the child's accomplishments.

If a child is becoming frustrated with a puzzle, step in with suggestions that will allow the child the satisfaction of completing the puzzle independently. "I wonder if the piece will fit if you turn it around? This part of the puzzle is red. Can you find a red piece that will fit right here?" If the child no longer has the patience to keep trying, offer to work as a partner: "I'll put in a piece, then you can put in a piece. If we work together, I'm sure we can finish this one."

Give the child the responsibility of returning the puzzle to its proper place when it is finished.

Bible Teaching/Learning Opportunities ■ *Sharing/Helping:*
When your lesson's Bible aims involve sharing, kindness or helping, select puzzles with pictures of children demonstrating these kinds of behavior. In your conversation encourage the child to talk about what is happening in the picture and relate the action to Scripture truth. "The girl in your puzzle is using her hands to help. What is she doing? God made our hands to help."

Working with puzzles gives children opportunities to share, to help and to be kind.

"Maria, thank you for sharing your puzzle with Cory. Our Bible tells us to share what you have with others . . . . "

Bible verses for your conversation:
"Be kind to one another" (Eph. 4:32, NASB).
"Serve the Lord with gladness" (Ps. 100:2, *NASB*).
"Learn to do right" (Isa. 1:17).
"Hear the word of God and obey it" (Luke 11:28).

Church: During a unit of lessons that focuses on the church, provide several puzzles showing familiar church experiences. Talk about the scenes as well as other experiences children enjoy at church. If it is necessary to use some puzzles with other scenes, compare them with what is happening at church. "Eric, why does the boy in your puzzle look happy? What are some things at our church that make you happy?"

Bible verses for your conversation:
"Come together as a church" (1 Cor. 11:18).
"Bring a love gift." (See 1 Chron. 16:29.)
"We'll be glad to give" (Judg. 8:25).
"I am glad" (John 11:15).

HOME LIVING

The Home Living area offers an environment in which young children can relive home experiences. These activities provide a natural setting where a teacher can relate Scripture truth to the children's interest and experience.

The Home Living area allows the young child to practice Christian concepts, such as sharing, helping, taking turns and being kind. The child can express thankfulness to God before eating a "pretend" meal or putting the baby to bed.

By listening and observing at the Home Living area, you can gain new insight into what a child is feeling. Each child's actions reveal clues to his or her interests, abilities, view of self and level of understanding of the concepts being taught.

Toddlers and **two-year-olds** may be content to simply rock the baby, feed the baby or put the baby to bed. They may want to be the baby, sitting in the toy high chair or lying in the doll bed. They usually play alone, not really involving anyone else in the activity. Since their command of words is limited, they often use play as a means of expressing ideas.

During the years *three, four and five,* the child becomes more verbal and imaginative play becomes more complex. The child spends additional time at play and needs extra "props" such as dress-up clothes and other accessories. Pretending helps the child learn to interact with other children as those in the Home Living area adopt various roles to become a "family." Familiar experiences are relived again and again.

Materials ■ Equipment for the Home Living area should be child-size rather than doll-size. A must for every Home Living area (including toddlers) is a doll bed, sturdy and large enough for a child to lay in, several blankets, and an assortment of dolls (include representatives of more than one race). Avoid dolls with hair (they usually become beauty parlor rejects within a short time) and dolls with mechanical features such as eye-blinking, wetting, walking, talking, etc. Add a wooden stove and sink unit for twos through fives. Home Living furniture can be purchased from educational equipment firms or made from crates and boxes. Furnishings should include unbreakable dishes, empty food containers, pots and pans, a child-size broom and two telephones. Omit silverware or anything which suggests being put into small mouths.

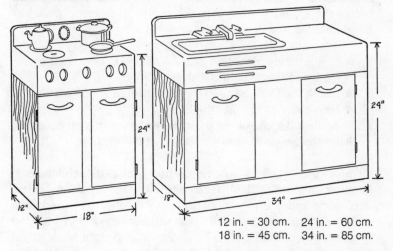

12 in. = 30 cm.   24 in. = 60 cm.
18 in. = 45 cm.   34 in. = 85 cm.

Dress-up clothes are an important part of Home Living play. Include dresses, men's and women's hats, scarves, jewelry, shoes and purses. Also jackets, neckties, a briefcase, discarded camera, binoculars, toolboxes, lunch boxes, billfolds and keys.

Dressing up will be easier if clothing is about a fifth-grade child's size rather than adult, although shoes should be large enough to go over the child's shoes. Other equipment that may be provided includes doctor and nurse kits for playing hospital, as well as toy cash registers and play money for playing store.

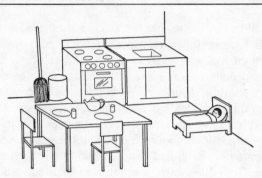

Procedure ■ Arrange the materials in the Home Living area before the children arrive. Then you should become an interested observer, moving into the activity to:

- ■ Suggest play ideas that provide natural connections to the lesson's Bible teaching/learning aims.
- ■ Relate the Bible aims to the child's interest and activity.
- ■ Help a shy child enter the activity.
- ■ Settle a dispute or aid the children in solving a problem.
- ■ Insure the safety and well-being of the children.

Since dramatic play is free and spontaneous, the children will become involved as their needs and interests dictate. A special accessory and a suggestion from the teacher can guide the child's play toward a specific aim without interfering with the spontaneous dramatic play. For instance, a picture book might become the stimulus to "read" to the babies at bedtime, allowing conversation about the unit's Bible stories. A small overnight bag and a suggestion about taking a trip can initiate extended play and opportunities to talk about God's care wherever we go.

As you plan for Home Living activities, ask yourself, "How will this activity help accomplish the lesson's Bible aims?"

In addition to dramatic play, the Home Living area is often the scene of simple food preparation activities. (See "Recipes" at end of book.) Banana pudding, no-bake cookies, lemonade or cheese slices are easy and popular. Many simple cooking experiences can be provided using electric fry pans. As children work with a teacher, many opportunities arise for emphasizing helping and sharing or God's care and provision for us.

Bible Teaching/Learning Opportunities ■ A teacher can use the young child's natural interest in Home Living activities to build many Christian concepts.

Helping: The Home Living area provides many opportunities for helping. The "children" help "Mother" set the table. "Daddy" helps iron clothes. "Everyone is helping in our home today. We have happy homes when everyone helps. Our Bible reminds us that we are helpers."

Children who work at the Home Living area are responsible to help put away equipment. "Michael knows just where to put the dishes. Cory is helping to pick up the dolls. What hard work she is doing! I am helping tuck the dolls in bed. Our Bible says, 'I will help.'"

> Bible verses for your conversation:
> "With love, help one another." (See Gal. 5:13.)
> "Help each other." (See 1 Peter 4:10.)

Thankfulness: As children play out familiar activities they can be guided to respond quite naturally in thanks to God for food, family, home, church, friends, etc. "What do we do before we eat our dinner? Shaun, you may tell God thank you for the good food. I saw a happy family in our 'home' today. God planned for us to have happy times with our families. We can tell God thank you for our families. Our Bible tells us to be thankful to God."

> Bible verses for your conversation:
> "I thank God" (2 Tim. 1:3).
> "Give thanks to God" (2 Thess. 2:13, *NASB*).
> "You are my God, and I will give you thanks" (Ps. 118:28).

ART ACTIVITIES

"What did you learn today in Sunday School?" Danielle's mother asked. Soundlessly, Danielle thrust a rumpled piece of paper at her mother. Danielle hoped her art work could speak for her.

Art experiences are among the most familiar—and most misunderstood—in an Early Childhood department. Most young children are introduced to crayons very young, but few adults take the time to observe the child at work, to see the real value of what is being done.

The key word in a young child's art experience is *process*—not *product*. The work the child puts into the experience is of more value than the finished result. The skills and attitudes and understandings a child gains far over-shadow the piece of paper that adults often make the object of much attention. The emphasis in this section is on providing enjoyable and meaningful art experiences for children to do, rather than on clever or beautiful art objects for them to make.

Art activities allow the young child to express thoughts and feelings. A child may express happiness through using bright colors in a painting. A shy or inhibited child may express those feelings by making just a few timid strokes with one finger on a finger painting. An angry child may release negative emotions by pounding, squeezing or twisting clay. Every child needs a teacher who is friendly and understanding about his or her art work. Art activities help the child learn basic Christian concepts of sharing, taking turns, being kind and helping others. Art activities create opportunities to learn respect for the ideas and work of other children as well.

As a child uses art materials in a relaxed, creative way, opportunities for natural conversation are likely to come. These "teachable moments" often are the best opportunities to connect basic and vital scriptural truths to areas of the child's interest.

As in other areas of growth, the child progresses through a certain pattern of development in artistic expression. And, as in other areas of growth, each child passes through these stages at his or her own speed.

The *first stage* in artistic development is called the *manipulative* stage. This stage begins when the child first begins to use crayons, paint or clay. It is a time of exploration; a time of experimenting with materials. The child discovers what happens when a crayon moves across a piece of paper or when a piece of clay is squeezed. The child needs to explore how the materials look, smell, feel and taste.

Toddlers through threes are usually in this manipulative stage of development. Most young children will return to this stage when introduced to new materials for the first time. A child's work should not be considered "babyish" nor should you ever say, "Draw something nice. Don't just scribble!"

The *second stage* sees the child progressing to the *controlled* stage. The child enjoys a new awareness of being able to regulate materials. The child knows how to use glue to make materials stick together; clay can be patted into shapes or pinched into pieces. The child purposefully makes a line go a certain direction by moving the crayon a certain way.

Third, the child enters the *naming* stage. The child completes a piece of work and announces, "See my doggy." At first, you may be able to see no resemblance between the object pictured and what the child says it represents. However, as skills rapidly develop, eventually the resemblance will become apparent. Early in this stage the child begins to name a piece of work *before* it is created. This intent to make a man, a flower, a house is a powerful impetus to maturing skills.

Your role is to encourage the child to feel pride in the efforts expended at whatever stage the child may be. Comments such as, "I like the bright colors in your picture, Brandon," or "You certainly worked hard on your painting. You know about painting!" show your acceptance of a child's work.

Materials and Procedure ■ When you introduce a new art activity, demonstrate the use of materials. Then remove your work. Some children might tend to copy your efforts and thus miss out on using their own creativity.

Painting: An apron or a smock is a must for all painting activities. An apron can be made from shower curtain materials. A smock can be made easily from a man's shirt. Cut off the sleeves to make them the right length for a child. The child wears the shirt backwards so it buttons in the back. Fix one large button and buttonhole so children can help each other. Since only a few children at a time will be painting, only several aprons or smocks are needed.

Sponges and soapy water for cleanup are also necessary for all painting activities.

Be sure the floor surface is washable. If it is carpeted, place a large plastic dropcloth or several thicknesses of newspaper on the floor in the painting area.

Materials for *finger painting* include finger paint and a smooth surface on which to paint. Finger paint may be purchased, but can also be made easily and inexpensively by mixing equal parts of liquid starch and soap flakes; add a few drops of detergent. Beat together till smooth. Then add tempera paint for color. The surface on which to paint can be finger paint paper, slick butcher or shelf paper, a formica or enamel tabletop, a large tray or a piece of oil cloth. One attractive feature of finger painting is that the entire creation can be wiped out in a moment if the child desires. Most children enjoy simply moving the paint around on a smooth surface and do not feel the need to make a picture.

If a child wants a picture to take home, lay a clean piece of paper over the finger painting, rub the paper lightly and pull it off. The child can then continue working on the original surface.

Toddlers and twos can be introduced to finger painting. Work with one or two children at a time to avoid messes. Expect some children to be reluctant to try until they have watched others for a while.

Provide pans of warm, soapy water for cleanup. Let the child soak his or her hands in the water for a few minutes when the painting is finished. Hands will come clean with very little scrubbing and children will enjoy the feel of the warm water.

For *brush painting,* provide paper, large brushes, liquid tempera and paint containers. Paper should be 18×24 inches $(45 \times 60$ cm). Newsprint, manila, butcher paper and the want-ad section from the newspapers can all be used. Brushes should have long handles—about 10 to 12 inches (25 to 30 cm)—and wide, soft bristles. Liquid tempera paint, available from art supply stores or educational material firms, is convenient and easy to use. It can be thinned with water, liquid starch or liquid soap, if necessary. Powdered tempera is less expensive to buy, but it is also less convenient, since it has to be mixed into a liquid. Powdered tempera can be mixed with water or liquid starch or a combination of both. The prepared mixture should be the consistency of heavy cream. A few drops of liquid soap added to the paint makes cleanup easier. Paint containers can include empty frozen juice or soup cans, baby food jars with screw tops or ½ pint milk cartons with the tops removed. The lids on baby food jars keep the paint from drying out overnight. The children can paint on tables or on walls protected against drips.

Twos should begin with only one color. As their experience with brush painting increases, the number of paints they use may increase. *Four and fives* may use from six to eight colors, with a brush for each color. The child needs a demonstration of how to drag the brush along the edge of the container to prevent dripping and to return the brush to the same color each time. You may have to instruct children to paint on the paper, not on hands, neighbor, the walls, etc. Except for these guidelines, each child should be allowed to paint what he or she wishes without pressure to produce a specific object.

Giving a child a picture or model to copy or "touching up" the child's painting creates feelings of dissatisfaction. Avoid questions and statements such as, "What did you paint? Do people have purple hair? Grass is green, not pink! This is how to make a rabbit." Such comments show a lack of valuing or understanding of the child's work. Accept a child's work as an expression of valid thoughts and ideas. Offer positive comments such as, "You have pretty bright colors in your picture. God made our eyes so we can see (red) and (blue) colors. Would you like to tell me about your painting? What are you thinking about as you paint?"

Children are expected to clean up their work area when they are finished. Even a two-year-old can wipe up drips with a damp sponge or cloth.

Dry paintings by hanging them on a small clothes-drying rack. Or, hang a fishnet or several strands of clothesline along one wall. Attach wet paintings with clothespins. Paintings become an added room decoration.

Materials for *gadget printing* include paint, paper, a variety of gadgets, paper towels and shallow containers such as foil pans. Paint and paper are the same as those used for brush painting. Gadgets can come from several sources. From the kitchen use forks, cookie cutters, a potato masher, sponges, tubes from paper towels; lemons and oranges cut in half; potatoes or carrots with a design cut in the end. Use empty spools from the sewing basket. Your gadget collection might also include erasers, pipe cleaners, corks, small plastic bottles, hair rollers, corn husks and pieces of sponge held by clothespins.

Dampen and fold two or three paper towels together to form a pad slightly smaller than the container in which the towels will be placed. Pour paint on the pad and allow it to soak in. The child presses a gadget on the pad and then onto the paper. To simplify cleaning gadgets, soak them in warm, soapy water.

String painting is an interesting variation of gadget painting. Clip a clothespin to one end of a piece of string. The child dips the string in paint, then drags it across the paper. The process can be repeated several times.

Spot painting requires a muffin tin, white powdered detergent, tempera paint, plastic spoons and white construction paper. Half-fill with detergent several cups in the muffin tin. Add enough tempera paint and water to make a gravy-like consistency. Place a plastic spoon in each tin. Fold pieces of paper in half. The child opens the paper and places spots of paint on one side. The child folds the other half on top and presses gently. When opened, a print appears.

Playdough/Clay: Clay and various types of play dough are excellent manipulative materials for young children. Children enjoy helping to make dough before using. (See "Recipes" in back of book.) Clay and dough must be kept in airtight containers to prevent drying out.

The tabletop should be covered when working with clay. The reverse side of oilcloth taped to a piece of heavy cardboard makes an ideal clay board. Aprons should be worn when working with clay. Sponges are needed for cleanup.

Working with clay requires more hand strength than most twos and younger threes possess; salt/flour dough is better suited to their ability. Give each child a piece of play dough about the size of a small grapefruit. In the manipulative stage, encourage the child to push, poke, pound, pull, smash and pat the dough. This gives ideas in how to use it. Timid children may shy away from this and other "messy" activities. Never force a child to do an activity. Allow the child to watch the other children, until he or she feels willing to try. Fours and fives enjoy using rolling pins, ice cream sticks and cookie cutters to roll and cut dough.

Each child should help clean the work area and tools with a damp sponge. A dustpan and brush are needed to clean up dry crumbs of dough. Before returning the dough to its airtight container, ask the child to roll it into a ball.

Cut and Paste: For cut and paste (or glue) activities, provide scissors, paper and paste or glue. Scissors should be about four inches long with blunt points. Be sure they cut easily to avoid frustrating children who are just learning to use them. Provide three or four pairs of left-handed scissors. Tie a string around the finger grip to easily identify the "lefty" scissors.

Cut and paste is best suited for older threes, fours and fives. The use of scissors depends upon the development of the small hand and arm muscles. Threes and even some fours are not skilled with scissors. When a child is having a hard time cutting, hold the paper tightly and let the child concentrate on cutting it. Provide scraps of paper which children can use to practice their cutting skills. They often enjoy tearing the paper rather than cutting it. Twos enjoy pasting precut pieces.

Paste or glue should be put in small containers for the child's convenience. Glue bottles must be tightly closed and wiped clean to prevent clogging. Use ice cream sticks or cotton swabs to apply paste or glue. And fingers are fun, too. The child can apply the glue or paste to the large background paper, then press the smaller piece onto that spot. Glue sticks can also be used.

Children need freedom to experiment with cut and paste activities just as they do with other art materials. At first the child seems to pile the cut pieces of paper on top of each other using big globs of glue or paste to stick them together. Also, the child may paste pieces so they extend over the edge of the background paper. Refrain from changing the child's work or suggesting where to paste the pieces. But don't be afraid to control the amount of glue or paste used!

For five-year-olds, cut and paste can evolve into a *tissue lamination* project. Provide tissue paper in two or three different colors for this activity. A piece of card stock or heavy paper can be used as a background. The child cuts or tears colored tissue paper into various sizes and shapes. The child then "paints" the background paper with liquid starch or diluted white glue. A wide paintbrush (two or three inches wide) will do this job quickly. Next, the child lays the tissue paper on the background. The child completes the process by brushing over the tissue paper with a small amount of starch or glue. If the tissue gets too wet, the colors may run together, creating interesting effects. Tissue may also be glued on other material such as cottage cheese containers, and cardboard tubes. Sometimes tissue paper is hard for even five-year-olds to cut. Be sure to have extra precut pieces available.

Children should be encouraged to put paper scraps back in the box when finished. A damp sponge is needed to wipe glue or paste off the tables and fingers. Sort through the scrap paper box periodically to remove any faded or soiled construction paper.

Collage: Collage is an arrangement of articles and objects glued together onto a background surface. Materials for collage can be as varied as your imagination. Include pieces of fabric, lace, paper, buttons, rickrack, string, carpeting, macaroni, straws, cotton, beads, burlap or string, foil, yarn, colored rice, beans and peas. From outdoors gather feathers, dried weeds, seeds and seed pods, twigs, seashells, leaves, lichen, sand or gravel.

The child will need white glue or paste and a piece of heavy paper or lightweight cardboard (approximately 12×18 inches [30×45 cm]) on which to glue the materials. Cardboard makes a good background since some materials are too heavy for paper. Scissors will be needed to cut some of the materials.

Making a collage stimulates a child's imagination and adds to a sense of achievement. Any combination of materials can be interesting. This is an activity at which every child can succeed because there is no right or wrong way to assemble a collage. Let the child enjoy experimenting with the materials. Avoid comparing one child's work with that of another.

Place collage materials in one or two shallow boxes or cake pans so a child can easily see and reach them. Select items that have some relationship to each other; for a creation lesson, use a variety of leaves; another time have things used for sewing (yarn, buttons, material scraps).

Making choices from too wide a selection is confusing, causing children to lose interest. Occasionally use backgrounds other than sheets of paper: paper plates and cups, fabric pieces, or large, empty cans.

Drawing/Coloring: For coloring activities provide large sheets (12 × 18-inch [30 × 45-cm]) of paper (newsprint, butcher paper, shelf paper or the reverse side of wallpaper or wrapping paper) and large crayons.

Large or jumbo crayons are easily held by young children. Some crayons should have the paper removed so the child can use the sides of the crayon. Periodically sort out and discard short, unusable crayons.

The young child does not need outlines such as found in coloring books. These predetermined shapes set a standard the child cannot reach, undermining creative development and self-confidence. Also, the young child's small muscle development does not allow him or her to color within the lines as expected in coloring books.

Crayon resist is done by brushing watercolors or thin tempera over a crayon drawing. The water runs off the wax crayon and the design or drawing stands out.

Fours and fives enjoy *crayon rubbings.* Gather objects such as leaves, coins or pieces of varying textured fabric. Fold a large sheet of paper in half. Place an object inside the paper. The child rubs the side of a crayon over the object, holding the paper still with the other hand. The outline and texture of the object appear on the paper.

Bible Teaching/Learning Opportunities ■ NOTE: Young children tend to concentrate fiercely while working on some art projects. In such cases, conversation is best saved for after they are finished.

Sharing/Kindness: Because most Early Childhood art projects are individual efforts, not group projects, teachers must plan carefully to create situations in which children interact with each other. One effective approach is to call attention to the necessity for the children to share materials and wait turns. As children work, identify specific acts of cooperative behavior. "Sara is sharing her sponge with Manuel. Our Bible tells us to 'share with others.' You are a kind helper, Justin. Thank you for picking up the spilled crayons. Thank you for sharing your paint with Erin, Jeremy. Our Bible tells us to help each other. Jeff, you may put the brushes in the water to soak. Amy may throw the newspapers away. I will put the paint on the sink. When we help each other we clean up very quickly."

Extend the child's learning by writing on the paper an account of a way he or she was kind, or a Bible verse you discussed together.

> Bible verses for your conversation:
> "Help one another." (See Gal. 5:13.)
> "Share with others" (Heb. 13:16).

Creation: Collages using nature items are easy for conversation about creation: "You have a seed pod on your collage, Katie. God planned for seeds to grow in seed pods. The seeds blew away. Now the pod is empty. It looks nice on your collage." Other activities call for focusing on the God-given skills the child is using in doing the project.

"God made your hands just right for finger painting, Colin. It is God who has made us. Clay is a special kind of dirt. God made the dirt. All things were made by God."

While three children finger-painted, Mr. Rivera sang softly, "Jennifer has hands that can paint, paint, paint. Brandon has hands that can paint, paint, paint! Lee has hands that can paint, paint, paint! God has made our hands!"

> Bible verses for your conversation:
> "God made the world." (See Acts 17:24.)
> "There is nothing too hard for God." (See Jer. 32:17.)
> "It is God who has made us," (Ps. 100:3).

Effective Storytelling

Storytelling can take place anytime during the morning, but especially during Bible Story Time (Sunday School) and Surprise Time (Churchtime).

Storytelling, a teaching method centuries old, has many values for the young child. It helps the child learn to listen and thus increases attention span. Listening to stories helps develop the child's ability to retain a sequence of ideas. It gives experience in speaking and helps increase vocabulary as the child talks about story events and people. Storytelling becomes most valuable for young children when it reinforces and coincides with firsthand experiences from the child's life.

One purpose of storytelling in the Sunday School is to share the gospel of God's love and the effect of this love on the child's life. Therefore, tell Bible stories that reflect a bit of the child's own everyday experiences. The world of a young child involves experiences with home, family, a few animals, nature, church and modes of travel. Bible stories must be based on some part of this familiar experience in order to begin with something he or she knows.

In addition to stories from the Bible, present-day stories are an effective teaching tool for communicating Scripture truths to young children. Children respond to stories about children their own age who do things they enjoy. These stories should always reinforce the basic truth of the Bible story told that morning.

The attention span of many *toddlers and two-year-olds* does not enable them to sit with a group to listen to a story. Therefore, briefly tell the Bible story many times throughout the morning whenever one or more of the children show an interest. Even when twos are able to participate in group experiences this practice should continue. Young children need—and like—to hear the story again and again. Remember that for toddlers and twos the "story" does not require much action or plot. A clear account of a simple event is all that is required. Give them just one idea and one person to identify.

A *three-year-old's* attention span allows listening to stories up to about three minutes long. However, most children under four will not be able to recall the sequence of actions in a narrative. They are able to recall the main focus of the story if it is clearly emphasized. *Fours and fives* can listen up to five minutes and are becoming able to retain the flow of the narrative.

Materials ■ The most important piece of equipment needed for Bible storytelling is your Bible! Keep it open so the children recognize it as the source of your story. Your Teacher's Manual is also important, but use it for study during the week, not on Sunday morning. Visual resources such as pictures, Bible story flannelgraph figures and puppets can be used to visualize a story. These resources reinforce and give meaning to your words. For a child who has never seen a sheep or a well, pictures are essential to learning. Visuals can be held in your hand, laid on the table or floor or placed on a flannel board. The flannel board should be small enough that you can easily hold it in front of you, thus giving children one focal point for their attention.

Preparation ■ Begin your story preparation early in the week. Read the story from the Bible. Read it again from a modern translation. Avoid the temptation to skip reading the story in the Bible "because I know it so well."

Next, read the story in your Teacher's Manual. This will help you tell the story in words the child will understand. It is also a guide for the use of specific visual resources. Notice the teaching/learning aims printed at the beginning of the lesson. This indicates the major emphasis the curriculum writers have taken in preparing the story.

Several times during the week practice telling the story and using the visual resources. You may find it helpful to make an outline on a small card to put in your Bible. Know the story well enough so you can look directly at the children most of the time.

To help children be able to remember the story, build your outline around these five essential story parts:

1. Setting

Where did this story take place? While young children will not benefit from attempts to pinpoint the geographical or historical location of a Bible story, they do need to be able to visualize something about the surroundings: a house, road, city, country-side, etc. A picture is very helpful in enabling children to mentally locate the story as having happened in a real place, not in a vague, perhaps imaginary, locale.

2. Main Character

Young children also need to be introduced to a central person in the story. If the character has a difficult name, it is helpful to let children practice saying the name before you get into the story: "Today we are going to hear a story about a very good king named Hezekiah. Let's practice saying Hezekiah."

It is always helpful to show a picture (or flannelgraph figure or puppet) of the main character.

3. Beginning Event

A story is not really a story unless something happens. The beginning event is the something that moves the main character to action. In most stories, the beginning event is a problem faced by the main character.

4. Action

The main story action is what the main character does in response to the beginning event. In many Bible stories, the main character will engage in a series of actions (e.g., Moses' actions in leading Israel through the wilderness). However, most young children find it difficult to follow a complex narration.

5. Result

What was the conclusion of the main character's efforts? What did the main character learn? What lesson do we learn from this? Unless you make a very clear summary statement, children will not recall the focal point of the story.

Procedure ■ During the Bible Learning Activity which you lead, look for opportunities to say something like, "What you just did reminds me of a Bible story. Would you like to hear a story?" If the child is interested, tell the story then. There is no need to fear reducing interest during Bible Story Time. Young children like stories best when they are familiar. At Bible Story Time, follow these guidelines:

1. Focus on Relationships

Young children need a meaningful relationship with their teacher more than they need to see a polished performance. If possible, place children in small (up to six children) story groups. This arrangement allows the teacher to establish and maintain eye contact, helping each child to feel the story is being told "to me." This also makes it easy for children to see any visuals that will be used. If the story must be told in a large group, teachers should be seated among the children to demonstrate their interest in what the children are hearing.

2. Capture Interest at the Start

The first few moments are crucial to the impact of the story. To make sure your children are ready to hear the story:

■ **Lead a simple finger fun poem or action song to help children focus on you.** If children are restless or distracted, it does little good to exhort them to turn around, sit still and pay attention. If you want their attention, do something to earn their attention. It also helps to remove any potential distractions (toys, books, purses, etc.) from the immediate area.

■ **Connect the story to an experience the children have shared.** Mention something that happened during the Bible Learning Activities which relates to the story you are about to tell. Or talk about something you know is familiar to everyone in your group.

■ **Introduce any unfamiliar aspects of the story.** While this should have been done during the Bible Learning Activities, it is helpful to take a moment to make sure children have some understanding of the setting and/or customs involved. If the story deals with a well, make sure the children know what a well is. If the story deals with travel, touch on ways people traveled in Bible times.

■ **Clarify why the story is worth hearing.** Give the children a reason—one that is important to them—for listening to your story. Your reason should have something to do with the purpose of the story, not just with an item of curiosity. How will the child benefit from knowing what this story teaches?

■ **Assume the children are interested.** Interest begets interest. If you are positive about the story, the children will be drawn to hear it. Even if children have heard the story before, tell them that you have heard it many times, it is one of your favorites and you hope it is one of their favorites also.

3. Use Normal Speech Patterns

Avoid talking down to children or making the story sound like either a fairy tale or a solemn declaration about the end of the world. Speak clearly, distinctly and slowly, but avoid the speech mannerisms people often adopt when talking to someone they think cannot hear or understand. As you talk, look for points where you can add extra expression for emphasis or variety:

■ **Try whispering** when you come to a crucial point in the narrative. A whisper is the most dramatic sound the human voice can utter.

■ **Vary your speaking rate**—speeding up or slowing down—in order to convey importance or secure attention. An occasional pause is very effective in creating suspense:

"The shepherds hurried down the streets of Bethlehem.
Faster and faster they walked.
When they came to the stable (pause)
    they went inside.
They saw Mary and Joseph.
And in the manger, they saw (pause)
    the baby Jesus."

■ **Add sound effects** if appropriate.

■ **Use repetition and action verbs, adding gestures when they fit.**

"Peter's friends helped him pull in the heavy nets
    filled with fish.
Pull . . . pull . . . pull!
They used their strong arms to pull the nets."

Pretend to pull the net as you describe the men's efforts.

■ **Use dialog** whenever possible. Instead of saying that Abraham told Lot he could have first choice of the land, give the story characters actual lines of dialog: "Abraham said to Lot, 'Look over all this land, Lot. You may choose first where you want to live.'" Put yourself into the place of each character and speak (and even act) as they would. For example, bend over slightly and pull a shawl over your shoulders as you tell the story of the widow who gave all she had.

■ **Use facial expressions to convey emotions.** Smile when telling about good things. Look angry or frightened or sad when that is how a story character might have felt.

4. Have Your Bible Open

Young children assume that "story" means "make-believe." They will not accept a Bible story as true unless you make a point that the story comes from the Bible and that the Bible is a true book. Show the place in your Bible where the story is located. (Some teachers like to highlight the story in their Bible and insert a picture, such as those commonly used in take-home papers, onto the facing page.)

5. Focus on the Main Point

If the children remember only one thing about the story, it should be the Focus statement (see your curriculum) for the lesson you are teaching. If you try to include too many details, too many characters, too many incidents, the child is likely to remember none of it, no matter how interesting you think it all may be. Unless you deliberately target your story toward that Focus statement and clearly state what the main point of the story is, your children will not be able to tell what the story is about. Avoid lengthy applications and comments after the story. Make the main point clearly and simply and then stop!

6. Keep It Brief

A good rule of thumb is to tell one minute of story for each year of the child's age. If you teach two-year-olds, a two-minute story is ample. For five-year-olds, anything longer than five minutes is stretching the limits of their attention span. It is better to briefly tell the story several times during the session than to have one longer story presentation.

7. Protect the Narrative Flow

Try not to interrupt the story sequence, for many children will have a difficult time picking up the thread again.

- Ask and answer questions before starting the story or after it is finished.
- Have children participate in telling the story or acting it out only after they are familiar with it.
- If behavior problems occur, have someone (Department Leader/Secretary) who is not telling the story, ready to move in and deal quietly with the problem, allowing the storyteller to continue.

Using Music for Learning and Fun

Of all the words spoken in your department on Sunday morning, the ones children will remember the longest are the ones set to music. Melody and rhythm give words great impact, making them easy to remember and repeat. Thus, music is one of a teacher's most powerful tools and should be carefully planned to support Bible aims. Songs should be chosen because they clearly and simply say what the child should remember after the session. Symbolic songs have no place in Early Childhood.

BENEFITS OF MUSIC

Music is a natural expression of feelings and experiences. A child who feels secure and relaxed will often sing or hum spontaneously in the midst of play. Through music a shy child can become involved in group activity; an overstimulated child can be helped to relax; an overactive, aggressive child can release tensions in an acceptable way.

Observe a group of children involved in play and you will notice that they make up their own songs, chants and games as they play. They respond to the rhythm of a swing, a jump rope or the wind. Music is an outlet for this creativity and a means of self-expression. With the aid of music a child can become a horse or a butterfly, an elephant or a clown. The child can use hands, feet or the whole body to express feelings the music creates. Through music the child can work off extra energy and stretch large muscles in acceptable ways.

Music can help children get acquainted and establish friendly feelings. Simple musical games using the child's name can help the child feel accepted. As the children gathered together for group time, Mrs. Martin began to sing, "I'm glad we are together .... There's Ashley and Brandon and Ryan and Lindsey .... " Hearing his or her own name helped each child feel an important part of the group.

Music provides the child with opportunities to respond to God in thankfulness and love. As the children looked at a snow-flake through a magnifying glass, Mrs. Lee softly sang, "Thank you, God, I thank you, God. Thank you, God, for snowflakes."*

A child under three will usually just watch and listen as you sing. A **two-year-old** who has heard a song several times may begin to respond by singing an occasional word or phrase with you. When the song includes actions, the child will often respond with a few of the motions. Children enjoy hearing the same songs again and again.

The **three-year-old** is beginning to sing with the teacher, though often a few words behind. The child enjoys singing famil-iar songs and will often ask, "Sing it again." Threes enjoy action songs and simple rhythm activities, even though they cannot yet keep time accurately.

Fours and fives enjoy singing with other children. They like using simple rhythm instruments. Fours and fives can make their own simple songs about what they've seen or done. Most fives have the ability to sing words and do motions at the same time.

There is no "song service" in a department for young chil-dren. Rather, music is used naturally and informally to help chil-dren learn specific Bible truths.

Materials ■ You already possess the most important piece of basic equipment—your voice. Add to that a knowledge of songs appropriate to your Bible aims, and you are ready to use music. Remember that your interest, enthusiasm and your familiarity with the songs are far more important than a professionally trained voice.

Songs for the young child should be short with repeating melody and lyric phrases. The songs should be rhythmic and have tunes which are easy to sing. Be cautious in using songs with symbolic lyrics or motions, for they communicate odd ideas to these literal-minded children. Many children's songs were written for older children who are better able to understand some types of symbolism. They are often popular because of their melodies, not because they effectively communicate ideas to young children.

Consider a young child's likely understanding of these lines in familiar children's songs:

"Climb, climb up Sunshine Mountain, faces all aglow." (It's hot work climbing up this hill.)

"I stand alone on the Word of God." (Here I stand, all by myself on top of this Bible.)

"Jesus wants me for a sunbeam." (Children have understood this one as being everything from string beans to kitchen appliances.)

"This little light of mine, I'm going to let it shine." (I'm going to walk around holding a candle/match/flashlight, etc.)

"I will make you fishers of men." (Obviously, I'm going to try to snag people with a fishing pole.)

"Deep and wide, deep and wide, there's a fountain flowing deep and wide." (This could be a drinking fountain which overflows or a large fountain in a park.)

Most songs fit into one or more of these three categories:

1. **Aim-related songs** ■ These are songs chosen to express and reinforce the Bible aims for your session. Choose songs which need a minimum of teacher explanation so the song can help you communicate clearly rather than you having to help the song. Select two to four aim-related songs to use each week throughout a unit of lessons. Sing a few songs several times each rather than singing several songs one time each.

2. **Activity songs** ■ These are songs designed to let children move parts of their bodies to get out the wiggles. Some activity songs involve movement of hands and arms and can be sung while children are seated. Others require the children to use their

entire body. At least one or two activity songs should be included in each Together Time to release energy, to prevent disruptive behavior and to recapture the attention of a restless group.

3. **Transition/Direction songs** ■ These songs simply put instructions to music, guiding children into the next segment of the session or to complete a necessary task. For example, at the conclusion of your Bible Learning Activities, you may begin singing,

"Tick! tock! Hear the clock.
It's time to put away our toys.
Tick! tock! Hear the clock.
Put our toys away."

Then as children begin to gather for Together Time, the leader begins to sing,

"How do you do, (Amy), how do you do?
How do you do, (Justin), how do you do?
We are glad that you have come,
We will have a lot of fun.
How do you do, (Megan), how do you do?"

All departments for young children need a sturdy, easy-to-operate cassette or record player and a selection of cassette tapes or records of aim-related and activity songs. Cassette or record players equipped with earphone jacks enable several children to listen to a tape without disturbing others.

Rhythm instruments are an important musical tool. Rhythm instruments can be purchased or made. They should include drums, wood blocks, bells, rhythm sticks, tambourines and shakers. Five-year-olds can make some of these rhythm instruments as a Bible Learning Activity.

Here are a few tips in using rhythm instruments:

1. Use them when children are together in one group, preferably seated in a large circle.

2. Demonstrate appropriate ways to use the instruments.

3. Begin playing music on your cassette player.

4. Distribute rhythm instruments, allowing children to begin

using them to accompany the taped music. Assist children as needed in using their instruments in a desirable manner.

5. At the end of a song, guide children in passing their instruments to the person on their left (or right), so everyone can use a new instrument in the next song.

6. Begin collecting instruments while the music is playing. Pick up the loudest instruments first, the one(s) with the quietest sound last.

Instrumental (piano, guitar, etc.) accompaniment is not necessary with young children, except to keep the teacher on pitch. You may want to consider an Autoharp. This simple stringed instrument can be mastered easily by anyone, regardless of musical ability. It is superior to a piano for accompanying young children's singing because its light tones do not overpower their small voices. Its compact size makes it adaptable for use, not only with a large group, but also in small group activities. Five-year-old children enjoy learning to play the Autoharp themselves. Even twos like to strum it while a teacher plays the chords.

Procedure ■ Babies especially enjoy being sung to. Teachers can sing simple songs while rocking, feeding or changing a child. A lullaby is an age-old tool for helping babies sleep.

With older children, at activity centers, be ready with songs related to the lesson aims. As the children plant seeds, you might sing softly, "Who made the seeds? God did . . . . " While children work with collage materials, you might comment that the children are using the hands God made for them; then sing, "Thank you, God. I thank you, God. Thank you, God, for my hands."

Music can be used during Bible Story Time to relate a Bible

story truth to the child's everyday experience. For example, at the conclusion of the story about Jesus calling His helpers, Mrs. Phelps used the Bible verse, "Come, learn of me." As the children completed invitations asking friends to Sunday School, the teacher said, "'Come, learn of Me. Come, learn of Me. Come, learn of Me,' Jesus said."

During Together Time, children and teachers sing together to reinforce learning experiences shared during Bible Learning Activities. In a lesson focused on responding thankfully for God's love, you might say, "I saw some children in the Home Living corner who were praying. They were thanking God for loving them. That made me want to sing a song about being thankful." The group then sings, "Be Thankful unto Him."

When children become restless or inattentive the wise teacher sings an activity song that allows the children to stretch and move tired muscles. Mrs. Kwan knew the children needed a change from quiet listening. So she began singing, "Let me show you how I clap my hands . . . . " The children began to sing with her. They sang the song several times using a variety of actions (stretching high, hopping and bending low). The concluding verse—"Let me show you how I sit tall . . . "—helped the children get ready for the next activity.

To introduce a new song use pictures or objects to illustrate the words. Let the children hear you sing the song (or play the tape) before you ask them to sing it with you. Suggest that five-year-olds listen for a certain word or phrase as you sing. Never ask children to "sing as loud as you can."

A song will catch the attention of children more quickly than a spoken command. Announce cleanup with a song such as, "Let's put our toys away . . . I can help and so can you . . . . " While children put away materials, you might sing, "I can help pick up my toys . . . . "

Listening to music helps children relax during Rest Time. Interesting pictures may result when instrumental music is played while children finger paint. Babies and toddlers enjoy soft background music throughout their session.

Bible Teaching/Learning Opportunities ■

Creation: As children observe the wonders of God revealed in nature, music can enrich this learning experience. The children went for a walk on a warm spring day. They stopped to look at the blossoming trees and listen to the singing birds. As they looked and listened, the teacher sang, "God made our wonderful world . . . . "

As twos and threes watched fish in the aquarium, the teacher sang, "Who made the fish? God did . . . . "

Bible verses for your conversation:
"God loves you." (See John 16:27.)
"All things were made by God." (See John 1:3.)
"God . . . made the world and everything in it," (Acts 17:24).

Prayer: Music is a natural way for children to pray. A child may want to do so several times throughout the session. Children arranging a bouquet of spring flowers might sing, "Thank you, God. I thank you, God. Thank you, God, for pretty flowers."

The children were finger painting. Mr. Anderson said, "I'm glad God loves us and watches us. He's even interested in Brian's blue painting." As the children worked, Mr. Anderson sang, "God cares for you."

Bible verses for your conversation:
"It is good to praise the Lord," (Psalm 92:1).
"I will pray to the Lord for you," (1 Samuel 7:5).
"We know that God hears us." (See 1 John 5:15.)

*NOTE: All songs referred to in this book are from the songbooks *Fun-to-Sing, Little Ones Sing* and *Activity Songs for Young Children* (see Bibliography). They have been carefully selected to help young children learn basic Bible truths. The thoughtful teacher will learn and use these songs consistently to present God's Word in a variety of interesting and meaningful ways.

Discipline and the Young Child

We were sitting in the second row, waiting for the concert to begin. Our boys were being their usual model selves, patiently holding their hands in their laps, quietly anticipating the start of the music. Well, maybe not perfectly patient, and not totally quiet, and their hands occasionally drifted out of their laps. But compared to the two boys in the front row, ours were indubitably angelic.

For the past ten minutes the front row had been the scene of mortal combat. It began somewhat innocently with a nudge and a poke and a giggle. That quickly led to a push and a shove and a grunt. Which of course escalated to a jab and a yank and a few words I had never heard from children so young.

In between rounds, the boys' mother bravely stepped into the fray, first with words of caution, then with warnings and next with threats of great severity. But each cease-fire was short-lived, and the ensuing strife was more vigorous than before.

The mother was the first casualty of the battle in the front row. Retreating in defeat, she wearily explained her new strategy to my wife: "I'll just let them get it out of their systems. They'll either get tired or someone will get hurt. Either way, they'll stop."

Perhaps it was fortunate that, in an auditorium filled with children, the din from that battlefront was not readily heard over the loud, lively music that we had come to hear. But I could not help wondering how that mother's approach to discipline was going to fare as her boys grew older.

Effective discipline has always involved two major areas of concern for parents and teachers:

1. Preventing behavior problems.

2. Responding to behavior problems.

Before looking at those two areas, we need to focus first on defining which behaviors of children really are discipline problems. There are many things that children do which some adult somewhere will consider a problem behavior. One little boy was very puzzled by the continual hushing and shushing of his teacher, always accompanied by a reminder that, "We are in God's house and mustn't (make noise, laugh, run, talk, wrestle, chew gum, etc.)." Finally the little fellow asked the teacher, "Doesn't God like little kids?"

If excessive restrictions are placed on the normal activity of children, it is questionable whether any child will be able to respond positively to the truths we proclaim. Teachers need to understand the typical behaviors of young children and be eager to accommodate those behaviors as much as possible.

Obviously, some healthy activities of children are simply not appropriate with a group of children in a classroom. Teachers need to be ready to limit these activities in ways that do not make children feel they have done something evil. For example:

Running—"Running is good to do outside. Inside we need to walk so no one will get hurt."

Yelling—"Yelling is for outside. Inside we use our quiet voices so that everyone can be heard."

Talking—"I like to hear the things you say, but right now it is time for you to listen."

Knocking Down Blocks—"It's fun to knock down what you build. You can knock down what someone else builds only if that person says you can."

Wiggles—"I know it's hard to sit still. Let's use our hands and sing a song together."

Just because a child's action creates a problem for a teacher does not necessarily mean it is a problem behavior. The problem sometimes lies with the teacher who may have unrealistic expectations for children's conduct. If the child is able to listen and participate, if no other children are being disturbed, and if the behavior is not likely to evolve into something truly disruptive, there is probably not a real problem.

Preventing Behavior Problems

In looking back over more than two decades of experiences with groups of children, I have become convinced that 90 percent (maybe 87 percent or 92 percent—I was too busy enjoying myself to keep statistics) of behavior problems with young children occur for either of two reasons:

1. The child is bored.
2. The child wants attention.

When a teacher provides interesting things to do and ample personal attention, few real behavior problems occur. The teaching plan suggested in the other chapters of this book has been designed to help you take care of that first need. Arrange your room to encourage active participation in learning, come to class prepared with adequate Bible Learning Activities, schedule your session to incorporate a good balance of learning experiences, keep in mind the limited attention span and understanding level of the age group—and children will not be likely to be bored.

The second need, personal attention, needs to be met before the child decides to earn some attention through problem behaviors. Keep in mind that a child would rather have negative attention than no attention, then do all you can to ensure that each child receives an abundance of eyeball-to-eyeball, nose-to-nose attention from loving Christian teachers throughout the session. The child who feels loved is unlikely to willfully create problems—except for some occasional and typical efforts to test the limits, to see if you care enough to keep drawing the line.

Responding to Behavior Problems

Behavior problems in the classroom run the gamut from those happy actions which are simply out of their appropriate time and place to acts of willful defiance. Fortunately, the latter type tend to be very rare in the early years of life, even among toddlers and twos who stamp their feet and refuse to follow our most reasonable instructions. (The self-assertive toddler or two can be exasperating, but should not be treated like a perverse rebel. This child needs firm, loving demonstrations of the limits and a lot of patience in helping the child learn to make appropriate choices. Expect a great deal of trial and error learning in this process.)

The following suggestions present a range of appropriate responses to behavior problems. The first approaches are effective with minor disruptions. The latter actions are appropriate with more serious or repeated challenges.

1. Try an Indirect Approach

Indirect approaches are those that do not directly address the transgression, but which can effectively redirect a child away from negative actions toward the behavior you desire.

Positive Focus ■ When misbehavior occurs, it is often helpful to call children's attention to positive actions. For example, should two children start to poke each other as the group is gathering for Together Time, comment on those who are following directions: "I really like the way Stacy and Michael came right over and sat down. You look like you're ready to sing with me." Or, if a child keeps blurting out answers before others get a chance to respond, remind the group of the instructions you have given: "I'm calling on people who are being very quiet and who have their thumb on their chin. That's great, Brady! You're perfectly quiet and your thumb is on your chin!"

Be careful in accentuating the positive, not to do so in a way that puts down the ones who are not there yet. If you say, "Why can't you boys sit as nice and quiet as these girls?" you will just have pushed a segment of your class into a secret pact never to be caught dead doing anything "those girls" do.

Change ■ When children's behavior indicates that their attention is somewhere other than where you want it to be, the most effective approach is to change something you are doing to recapture their attention:

Change your speech. Slow down or speed up, get louder or softer, exaggerate the inflection on your words.

Change your posture. Lean forward, stand up, sit down, use a new gesture.

Change the activity. Lead the group in an activity song or finger fun or play a game. If you sense that the whole group is restless, quickly end what you are doing and start doing something else.

Ignore ■ If you sense that a child is doing something to get attention, the best response is to ignore it—if possible. If you respond, the child will have succeeded in getting your attention and will be likely to do the same thing again. Be aware that there are times when you cannot ignore a child. For example, the child may be doing something harmful or may be getting plenty of attention from the other children. But, when possible, ignoring attention-getting behavior is the best way to eliminate it, if plenty of positive attention is provided after the child stops the undesirable actions.

2. Try a Direct Approach

Some behaviors cannot be ignored, but neither do all behaviors require the identical response. These direct responses provide a teacher with some options in deciding what to do with a specific child in a particular situation. These options all involve the child.

Signal ■ Teachers have long used eye-contact as a powerful signal to catch a child's attention and redirect behavior. When a child becomes aware of being observed doing something known to be out of line, there is usually an immediate return to the correct behavior. Along with catching the chid's eye, some effective signals include a wink, a nod of the head, a smile (or frown) or a gesture (such as pointing towards where the child should be looking).

Using the child's name is the most commonly used verbal signal. This can be done in passing, simply inserting the child's name into the flow of your story or conversation. Since their names are the most important words in children's vocabularies, this simple procedure is very effective in drawing children's attention back in the desired direction. Sometimes, along with the name, a child needs to hear a simple instruction of what to do (see the section labeled "Instruction" in this chapter).

Another type of signal is used with the whole class to catch attention:

- Try slowly counting aloud with the understanding that children are expected to be quiet by the time you reach three.
- A flick of the lights or a chord on the piano can be the signal to start putting materials away.
- Slowly folding your hands and laying them in your lap (or bowing your head) can lead the group in following your example.

Signals usually need to be accompanied with a simple spoken direction. This direction may need to be repeated once or twice.

Touch ■ A gentle hand on a child's shoulder, a soft pat on the knee, a hand laid on top of the child's—these are effective ways to let a child know you are aware of what is going on and to help the child calm down and change behavior. Offering to hug or hold a child on your lap is frequently successful in helping the child feel loved and become desirous of cooperating.

In contrast, it is never appropriate in a Sunday School or Churchtime group to spank or slap a child. The potential negative impact on the child, the rest of the group and the teacher's relationship with parents can all outweigh any hoped for benefits—from corporal punishment. Other direct actions are far more effective in group situations.

Move ■ Sometimes, simply moving anywhere is effective in recapturing attention. It is also very helpful to move closer to a misbehaving child or to move away from a distraction.

At times it becomes necessary to move a child. This can be done without calling attention to what the child has been doing, simply by asking the child to do something for you (hold up a picture, point to an object, bring you an article, hand something to another child or teacher, etc.). Be careful in using this technique that you do not limit its use to those who cause disturbances. The ones who are cooperating need to be rewarded with opportunities to do things for you.

Sometimes you need to be more overt in moving a child. Usually this is needed when two or more children have been mixed together and have created an interesting chemical combination. At other times a child may simply be too far away from the calming influence of a teacher to be able to listen or participate productively.

Remove ■ When a child misuses materials, it may be necessary to remove the materials from the child or the child from the materials. The child who abuses another child—or the group—may need to be removed from that activity. This should not be done punitively: "You've been such a bad boy with the glue, you have to go sit in the Naughty Chair." It should be done firmly, but gently, with a simple explanation of what you are doing.

Time Out ■ When it is necessary to remove a child from an activity or from the group, try referring to it as a "time out" rather than as a form of punishment. "Jonathan, you need a time out for a few minutes. Sit over here and watch until you feel ready to help us sing again." The idea of a time out does not carry a stigma and it conveys the idea that the child will be allowed to return to action quickly. It also recognizes that a child's disruptive behavior is often the result of becoming tired or overstimulated. Pausing for a few moments can help a child regain both physical and emotional control.

A time out is very helpful when a child has become emotionally upset. Rather than trying to reason with an angry or frantic child, allow a few moments "space" in which the child can regather the shreds of lost composure.

Instruction ■ There are many times when it is appropriate to give a direct instruction to a child who is creating a problem. It is important to phrase a direction positively, telling a child what to do, rather than just what to stop doing. A vague command to "Stop bothering Billy," or "Quit causing trouble," is as difficult for a young child to obey as "Stop breathing!" Even a more specific instruction, such as telling a child not to wiggle, poke, talk, squirm, etc., is not very helpful for the child's learning unless accompanied by a clear statement of what the child is now expected to do instead:

- ■ "Rachel, it is time for you to listen quietly. You may talk when the story is finished."
- ■ "David and Ryan, you both need to fold your hands in your laps. I'll be watching to see how still you can keep them."
- ■ "Color on your own paper, Jennifer. Show me a good place you can put some color next."

Not only are positive directions easier for the child to obey, they sound friendlier and are more likely to elicit a cooperative attitude than will statements of restriction.

Behavioral instructions are most effective when accompanied by one or more of the other direct approaches. Children need to see us take action, not just use words. Directives and warnings are very ineffective when not backed up with firm, gentle action.

Explanation ■ Children need and deserve a simple, direct explanation of an action we take or an instruction we give:

- ■ "You can only build with blocks as high as your shoulder. I

cannot let you build higher or someone might get hurt."
- "I need you to pick up the puzzle pieces on the floor. If some pieces get lost it will spoil the puzzle."
- "You and Samantha need to take turns with the doll, Ashley. The toys in our room are for everyone to enjoy."

3. Try Dialog

When a behavior problem is repeated or is otherwise considered a serious problem, the child may need to be engaged in dialog about the situation. Dialog involves the child in talking and thinking about what has been done. It also helps the child learn to develop increased responsibility for his or her actions. Children need to be guided beyond simply doing what they are told (although that is an important aspect of development), to learning self control, understanding what is right and being able to do it. Obviously, dialog is only appropriate with children old enough to put their thoughts into words, thus it is of limited value with children under three years old.

The objective in using dialog is to draw out the reluctant child into honest, open conversation about what happened. Most children, when realizing they have been caught in misbehavior, tend to instinctively withdraw from interaction lest they say something that might incriminate them. Their limited experience in this world has taught them that any admission of guilt results in swift and immediate retribution.

The child who views the teacher as interrogator, investigator, prosecuting attorney and judge will not be likely to want to dialog. Therefore, the teacher must take pains not to play any of those roles, but rather to be a guide who helps the child learn a better way of behaving. The effective guide is one who has experienced and understood the truth of 1 John 1:9. ("If we confess our sins, he is faithful and just and will forgive us our sins and purify us from all unrighteousness.")

While human experience teaches that justice requires punishment as the response to confession, God dispenses justice to His children by providing forgiveness and cleansing in response to an admission of guilt. The child who sees love and compassion in the eyes of a teacher, and who has previously experienced that teacher's firm and loving guidance, will be able to talk openly about a problem and will be receptive to learning through the process.

Five questions are very helpful in guiding a child in dialog about a behavior problem:

1. "What happened?" (Or, "What did you do or see?") This question simply asks the child to tell what went on in a situation. A "What happened?" question is better than a "Why?" question ("Why did you hit him?") for three reasons:

- "Why" questions require that the child is capable of understanding and explaining motivation, a very sophisticated level of reasoning. A common response to a "why" question is a puzzled shrug or "I dunno."
- Asking a child to give a reason for doing something is asking the child to justify unacceptable behavior. In most cases this takes the form of blaming the other child: "'Cause he wouldn't give me the glue!" or "He hit me first!" are likely responses.
- "Why" questions are almost always phrased in an accusatory tone of voice. The adult is declaring the child guilty before the dialog begins, hardly an approach aimed at winning the child's trust and confidence.

Even if you saw the entire incident, there is value in getting the child to describe it. The "What happened?" type of question allows the child to begin talking, which automatically helps to release some of the tension the child may be feeling.

If the child cannot or will not tell what happened, you can offer your version of what you saw or heard and ask the child to agree or elaborate. Should the child plead innocence, it is not necessary for the teacher to become Sherlock Holmes and ferret out the truth of the mystery. Simply move on to the next question and deal with the matter as though it were a hypothetical discussion.

2. "What makes this (the situation just described) a problem?" This question leads the child to think about the results of misbehavior. It is far better to guide the child to think through the implications than for the adult to do all the thinking for the child. However, if the child is unable or unwilling to offer a reason, you must come through with a satisfactory, child-level explanation of why such behavior is unacceptable in this situation. The more specific the reason (e.g., "Hitting hurts and makes people mad at each other."), the better for the child's growing understanding.

3. "What should you do now?" Whatever the misbehavior, it does little good to dwell on what is past. Once there is a clear recognition of why that action is not appropriate, the child needs to be brought to the present moment, considering what could be done to resolve the problem. Even the child who professes innocence can be led to suggest practical steps to take to remedy a negative situation.

Some problems have an obvious solution. A mess on the floor needs to be picked up. A toy wrestled from another child needs to be returned (or put away if both parties cannot amicably resolve the matter).

Other problems are stickier because certain actions cannot be undone. Unkind words cannot be recalled. A poke or blow cannot be erased. A ruined art piece may not be restored. The most common suggestion of children in these cases is to say, "I'm sorry." The problem with that answer is that children come to view those words as a magical incantation which absolves them of all responsibility for their actions. Thus, the fourth question is often necessary to clarify matters.

4. "How would that help?" Would saying "I'm sorry" make the hurt go away or repair the damage done? Children need to know that a sincere apology can help by letting the other person know the action was accidental or is now regretted. But those words do not by themselves erase the misdeed. You may need to suggest some practical ways the offender can atone—and you may need to be involved in helping the child carry through on the remedial action. For example, a child whose feelings were hurt could be given a special privilege in the class (something the offender would have liked to do).

Both the offender and the "offendee" need to see that not all actions can be made right. This knowledge can be used as a further reason for learning to do things that are kind and helpful to each other.

5. "What would be better to do next time?" Especially in situations where the damage could not be reversed, children need to consider better courses of action to take the next time they face a similar situation:

- "What do you think you could do the next time someone else has a doll you want?"
- "How could you remember to be a good listener the next time we have a story?"
- "The next time you feel angry, how could you make sure you don't hurt someone else?"

In dealing with behavior challenges in your classroom, keep in mind that lessons taught this week may need to be patiently repeated again in the weeks to come. In a once-a-week program, the days between sessions often erase from a child's memory the truths you felt were so vividly communicated last week. It is easy to become frustrated with a child who falls back into behavior problems, but teachers need to realize that if a child has spent five years learning to misbehave, those habits will not disappear in one or two sessions.

While you should not expect children to become angelic because you tell them to do so, you can expect that children will respond to your consistent, loving guidance. Even if the rest of their world is reinforcing negative behaviors, children with whom you build a relationship of love and trust will want to please you. Out of that desire—and the growing awareness of God's great love—will come the ability to begin living up to the example and instructions and explanations which you provide.

Although all teachers dream of a session with no behavior challenges, it is often the moment that you are helping a child resolve a problem that you are also communicating God's better way of living. When your goal reaches beyond simply stopping the child's disruptive activity, you will find many opportunities to help children see how God's love touches every area of our lives.

Bibliography

BOOKS

Campbell, Ross. *How to Really Love Your Child.* Wheaton, IL: Scripture Press, 1981.

Chamberlain, Eugene. *When Can a Child Believe?* Nashville, TN: Broadman, 1971.

Durkin, Lisa Lyons. *Parents & Kids Together.* New York, NY: Warner Books, 1986.

Elkind, David. *Miseducation: Preschoolers at Risk.* New York, NY: Alfred A. Knopf, 1987.

Haystead, Wesley. *Teaching Your Child About God.* Ventura, CA: Gospel Light, 1974.

Holm, Marilyn Franzen. *Tell Me Why: A Guide to Children's Questions About Faith and Life.* Minneapolis, MN: Augsburg, 1985.

Klein, Karen. *How to Do Bible Learning Activities: Ages 2-5.* Ventura, CA: Gospel Light, 1982.

Snowball, Marilyn. *Preschool Packrat.* Santa Barbara, CA: The Learning Works, 1982.

Ziglar, Zig. *Raising Positive Kids in a Negative World.* Nashville, TN: Thomas Nelson, 1985.

PERIODICAL

National Association for the Education of Young Children. *Young Children.* 1834 Connecticut Ave. NW, Washington, D.C. 20009-5786.

SONGBOOKS

Painter, Alice, Margaret Self, and Wesley Haystead. *Activity Songs for Young Children.* Ventura, CA: Gospel Light, 1983.

Self, Margaret M. *Fun-to-Sing Songs for Young Children.* Ventura, CA: Gospel Light, 1989.

_____. *Little Ones Sing.* Ventura, CA: Gospel Light, 1972.

Recipes

SALT-FLOUR DOUGH

Children enjoy the relaxation and unending variety of forms that come with molding, squeezing, rolling and pounding dough. This activity becomes even more fun when the children mix the dough themselves. Try these no-cook recipes for different textures:

Recipe No. 1

> 2 parts flour
> 1 part salt
> 1 tablespoon alum
> Add water and dry tempera to achieve desired consistency and color.

Recipe No. 2

> 4 cups flour
> 2 cups salt
> food coloring
> 1/4 cup cooking oil
> 1/8 cup soap flakes
> 2 cups water
> 1/8 cup alum

Recipe No. 3

> 1 1/2 cups flour
> 1 cup cornstarch
> 1 cup salt
> 1 cup warm water

Recipe No. 4 (Cooked)

1 cup flour
1 cup water and food coloring
1/2 cup salt
1 tablespoon cooking oil
2 teaspoons cream of tarter
Cook until consistency of mashed potatoes. Do not boil. Knead until cool.

With all recipes, if dough is sticky, dust with flour. If dough is stiff, add water. All recipes need to be stored in airtight containers. Recipe No. 3 hardens nicely and can be painted if sculptures are to be preserved.

PEANUT BUTTER CLAY

Peanut butter
Dry, powdered milk
Honey
Mix equal parts peanut butter and powdered milk. Slowly add honey to achieve desired thickness. If mixture is too sticky, add more milk.
Mold the "clay" into any desired shape. For added fun, decorate with seeds, raisins. Then eat it!

HOMEMADE PAINT

1/2 cup vinegar
1/2 cup cornstarch
Food coloring
Mix vinegar and cornstarch together. Add food coloring slowly as you stir, until desired color is reached. If paint is too thin add cornstarch. Add vinegar if too thick.

FINGER PAINT

Liquid starch
Soap flakes
Powdered tempera

Mix equal parts of starch and soap. Add tempera to achieve color desired. Add more starch if too thick, more soap if too thin.

FINGER WHIP

Soap flakes
Water
Beater
Mix equal parts water and soap flakes. Whip with beater. Add more water to thin, more soap to thicken.

PUD

½ box cornstarch
Water
Pour cornstarch onto shallow cookie tray. Add water slowly and stir. Pick it up. Squeeze it. Watch what happens!

BUBBLES

1 quart water
¼ cup Dawn liquid detergent
1-2 drops glycerin
Mix ingredients and place in large bowl or dishpan Let solution set several hours before using. Use plastic strawberry boxes, six-pack plastic rings, bent clothes hangers, etc. to dip into solution. If done indoors, place container on towels or newspapers to absorb water.

Giant bonus idea: Multiply ingredients by 4 and place in a child's plastic wading pool. Use a hula hoop to make a huge bubble!

HEALTHY SNACKS
CHILDREN CAN HELP PREPARE

Fresh fruit slices
Vegetable slices with dip
Banana dipped in sesame seeds
Cheese and crackers

Granola (try making your own)
Granola mixed with honey to make cookies
Fresh fruit salad
Sunflower seeds
Baked pumpkin seeds
Milk (mix equal parts whole milk with milk from powder to reduce cost)
Cereal mix (combine several dry cereals, mix with melted butter)
Fruit sandwich (fruit slices between crackers)
Yogurt (any flavor)
Stuffed celery (spread cream cheese or peanut butter, top with raisins or wheat germ)
Bible Time snack (mash dates, figs and raisins, form into balls, roll in graham cracker crumbs or wheat germ)
Yogurt milk shake (blend equal parts yogurt with fruit juice, plus some banana and honey for flavor)
Banana Delight (blend some banana, honey and 1/4 teaspoon vanilla with milk—vary proportions to taste)

SIMPLE COOKING RECIPES FOR HOME LIVING

Butter

3 tablespoons whipping cream
Salt (optional)
Baby food jar with lid

Place cream in jar. Shake cream until a ball of butter forms. This takes a lot of shaking! Pour off remaining liquid. You may sprinkle a little salt on the butter.

Individual Pudding

For each child:
1 tablespoon pudding mix (any flavor)
milk
1 baby food jar with lid
1 spoon

Put mix into jar. Fill jar 3/4 full with milk. Close lid and shake until pudding forms. Eat pudding from jar.

Pumpkin Pancakes

>   4 cups pancake mix
>   2 eggs
>   3 cups milk
>   1 cup cooked pumpkin
>   1 teaspoon cinnamon

Mix ingredients thoroughly. Cook pancakes in electric skillet (350 degrees). Serve dry or with butter and syrup.

Painted Cookies

>   1 or 2 cookies per child
>   4 egg yolks
>   4 colors of food coloring
>   4 bowls
>   4 CLEAN paintbrushes

Mix each egg yolk with 1-5 drops of food coloring to make a colored glaze. Brush glaze onto cookies.

Applesauce

>   4 medium cooking apples, peeled and cored
>   1 cup water
>   1/2 cup brown sugar, packed
>   1/4 teaspoon cinnamon
>   1/8 teaspoon nutmeg

Cut apples into quarters. Heat water and apples in electric skillet until water boils. Reduce heat and simmer 5-10 minutes, until apples are tender. Stir in sugar, cinnamon and nutmeg. Heat to boiling again. Let cool before tasting.

Fingerjello

>   4 envelopes unflavored gelatin
>   water
>   6 oz. package of any flavored gelatin

3 oz. package of lemon flavored gelatin

Dissolve unflavored gelatin in 1 cup cold water. Dissolve flavored gelatin in 4 cups boiling water. Mix the gelatins together. Pour into 9 × 13-inch (22.5 × 32.5-cm) pan. Refrigerate until firm. (Once it's firm, refrigeration is not needed.) Cut in squares and serve as finger food.